MINI WORLD MYSTERIES

SOLVE THE CLUES ... TAKE A RISK
BECOME A SLEUTH ... EXPECT A TWIST!

AGES 10 YEARS TO ADULT

© Copyright: Gary B Lewis 2025

All rights reserved. No part of this publication may be reproduced, stored in a retrieval system or transmitted in any form by any means, electronic, mechanical, photocopying, recording or otherwise, without the prior permission of the publisher / author.

EXEMPTION CLAUSE: The publisher hereby grants readers permission to photocopy or trace the graphical template pictures within this book — exclusively for use in solving the Mini World Mysteries.

Layout and design by Gary B Lewis

Lewis, Gary B, 1952—
Mini World Mysteries

1. Games & Puzzles—Fiction. 2. Family—Intergenerational Games I. Title.

ISBN: 978-1-76402-331-3

PUBLISHED BY GARY B LEWIS
Cranbourne East, VICTORIA 3977

www.gablesbooks.com

TABLE OF CONTENTS

INTRODUCTION — page 5

Casefile #1:
TABLE TALK MYSTERY — page 7

Casefile #2:
SCARECROW IN THE VEGIE PATCH MYSTERY — page 17

Casefile #3:
A WALK IN THE PARK MYSTERY — page 27

Casefile #4:
K-9 CAPERS MYSTERY — page 37

Casefile #5:
TEDDY BEARS' PICNIC MYSTERY — page 55

Casefile #6:
THE SECRET GARDEN OF KING AZUREPAW MYSTERY — page 71

Casefile #7:
HANGING OUT ONLINE MYSTERY — page 83

Casefile #8:
BUTTERFLY FRENZIE AT #54 MYSTERY — page 97

SOLUTION FILES — page 107

INTRODUCTION

Hey there! Welcome to the very first edition of MINI WORLD MYSTERIES. It's been a long time coming ... almost thirty-five years in fact! Not that I even planned on writing a book back in 1989, but that was the year when the ideas for these activities were birthed.

I was teaching a composite class of years 3 & 4 students, in which there was a small group who were very bright. Super smart readers. Top at Math and Spelling. They really kept me on my toes!

I needed to find a way to engage their logic, reading skills and problem solving initiatives. As a 'creative', my brainwave was to create some MINI WORLD SCENARIOS — actually I simply called them CASEFILES back then.

These activities were a real hit with this cohort of brainiacs. So much so, that I still have the originals — all hand written and drawn, as I was fairly computer illiterate back then. I designed six different CASEFILES.

'TABLE TALK', 'SCARECROW IN THE VEGIE PATCH' and 'A WALK IN THE PARK' were three of the originals, which I have revamped for this book. In total there are eight MINI WORLD MYSTERIES for you to solve. All the other scenarios have unfolded over the past few months.

These mystery scenarios are suitable for ages 10 through to 80 years of age. You read that correctly! Living in a retirement village as well as having teenage grandchildren, allows many opportunities to road test such ideas.

Earlier this year, I had another brainwave ... to create a 3-D mini world for 'TABLE TALK' to engage some of our neighbours. The activity was a hit! But as a 'creative tragic' whose wife also happens to be of like-mind ... one thing led to another ... and at the time of writing this book, we have created eight MINI WORLDS in 3-D! Unfortunately we've had to put a lid on our creative juices for the time being, basically because of lack of storage space!

This book has been specifically written for those who love a '*whodunit*' type mystery to solve. Obviously, it had to be written in 2-D format. For those interested in the 3-D presentations, you can see pictures of them on my website: www.gablesbooks.com . Just click on the BLOG tab.

Throughout this book you will find TEMPLATE PAGES which can be photocopied or traced and cut out. I suggest you use white card, otherwise laminate your paper printout for durability.

You can color them to brighten up the activity if you like. You could also store your cut-outs in an envelope for re-use with friends or family.

Once your cut out template is prepared, you will be ready to begin solving the linked mystery.

In each chapter you will be given a new MINI WORLD MYSTERY to solve. Each chapter includes a copiable template, explanation & scenario, clues and solutions.

If you are playing any of these activities as a group, nominate one person to be the narrator/adjudicator.

Finally, let me pay tribute to that cohort of brainiac years 3 & 4 students from 1989 ... thank you for the inspiration and challenge! And thank you to my dear wife, Maree of over 50 years, for your perpetual support and encouragement.

SOLVE THE CLUES ... TAKE A RISK
BECOME A SLEUTH ... EXPECT A TWIST!

Mini-World Mysteries
Chapter #1

"Table Talk Mystery"

- Your task is to discover who was sitting next to whom and opposite at the table just before a mysterious bomb scare occurred.
- Then solve the mystery of how the bomb scare occurred ... and who was involved.
- READ through each clue **_separately_** & **_carefully_** e.g.
- **NOTE**: You may need to go back and re-read some of the clues. You can solve this mystery as an individual or a team of up to four people.

TEMPLATE #1
'TABLE TALK MYSTERY'

On Over the next two pages you will find your B & W template for this **MINI WORLD MYSTERY**.

The pages can be photocopied or traced then cut out. Use white card, otherwise laminate your paper for durability.

You can also color them to brighten up the activity if you like.

Perhaps store your cut-outs in an envelope for re-use with friends or family.

Once your cut-out template is prepared, you will be ready to begin solving this mystery which starts on page 12.

You will be given the explanation, scenario, clues and solutions.

If you are playing this activity as a group, nominate one person to be the narrator/reader/adjudicator.

MINI WORLD MYSTERIES

Print/trace/copy this page Color

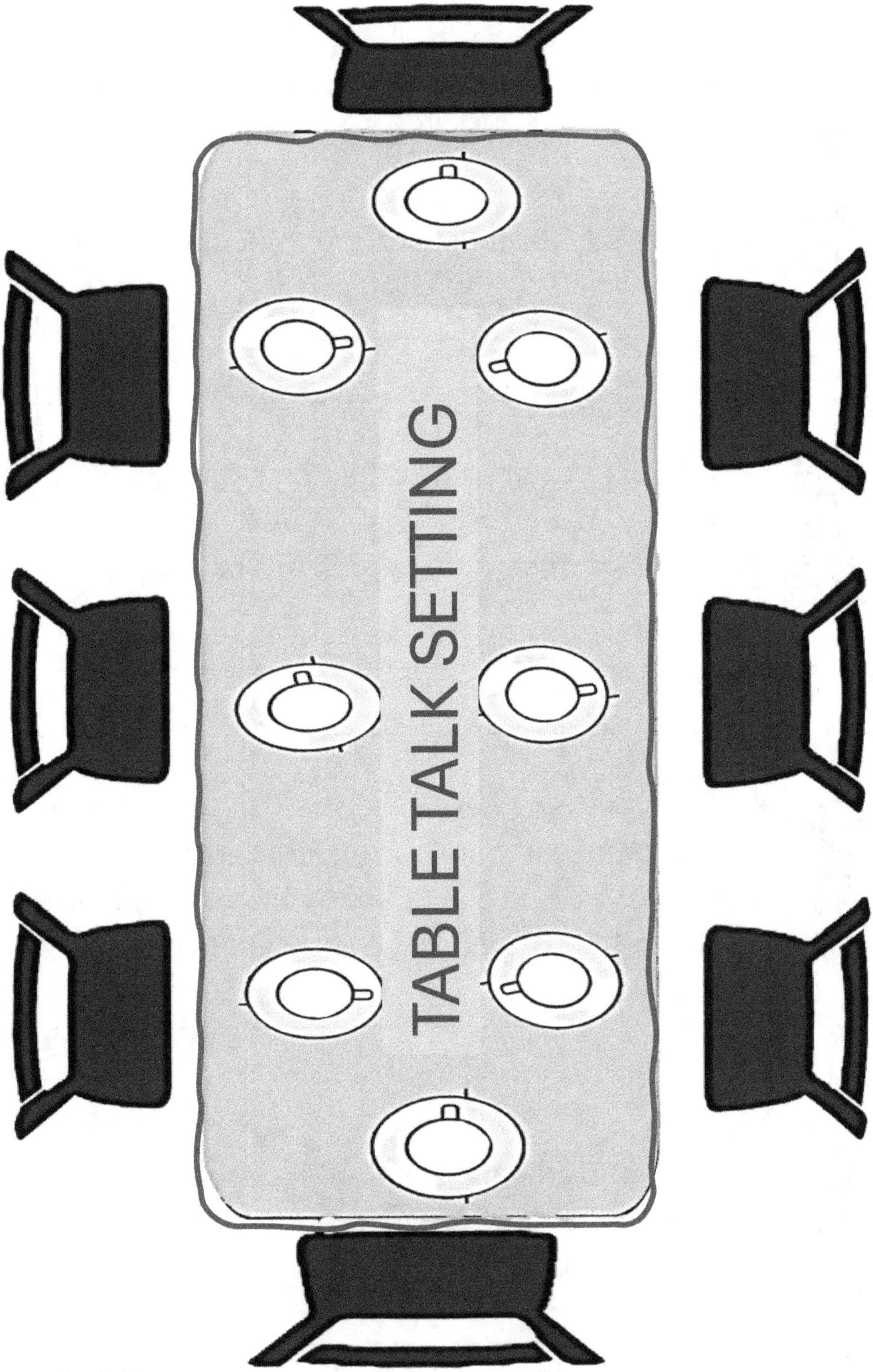

TABLE TALK SETTING

TABLE TALK MYSTERY

CLUES

CLUE 1

BILLY sat next to OLIVIA who was very chatty ... and directly opposite Ilish whom he rather fancied.

ILISH secretly liked Billy too, but she needed to get her 'BESTIE'S' approval.

CLUE 2

KELLIE did not sit next to BILLY who was a bit of a bully. She sat next to OLIVIA who talked a lot ... which meant that she didn't have to say much.

CLUE 3

TARA was sitting next to JOSH who was a bit of a joker. She was quite bossy and liked to embarrass people or just annoy them. So she sat opposite KELLIE whom she could tease by kicking her feet.

CLUE 4

JOSH sat to the right of Ilish. He sat opposite OLIVIA ... although she talked too much, she always laughed at his jokes.

MINI WORLD MYSTERIES

CLUE 5
OLIVIA did not sit next to Ilish or Tara, as one of them was a 'Queen Bee', and the other was a 'Wanna-be'.

CLUE 6
JOSH did not sit directly opposite BILLY or KELLIE. He sat where he knew everyone could hear his jokes.

CLUE 7
MISSY sat next to Ilish … and opposite ZOE so she could make a quick exit just in case she suddenly felt claustrophobic.

CLUE 8
ZOE actually didn't mind where she sat just as long as she could see the window. When the bomb scare occurred, she was sitting next to her friend KELLIE, who was very shy and rather sensitive to sudden noises.

CLUE 9 Amidst the normal chit-chat, and clatter of dishes and cutlery, the instigator of the bomb scare waited for just the right moment to act. This person took from their pocket a 'PARTY-POPPER' in anticipation ... and held it underneath the table ready to set off.

CLUE 10 Just before the bomb scare the **'Photographer'** had set up their camera to snap some photos of those at the other end of the table. The **'Photographer'** was standing between the **'Wanna Bee'** and the person nearest to the door.

CLUE 11 With precision timing, right after one of the **Joker's** funniest jokes, there was a brief moment of awkward silence ... which was immediately shattered by a loud explosion from underneath the table, followed by a flash of light in the room, screaming and a lingering smell of a foul gas.

MINI WORLD MYSTERIES

CLUE 12

Instantly ... the '**Queen Bee**' and the '**Wanna-be**' both squealed! '**The Talker**' and the '**Joker**' both cracked up laughing. The '**Bully**' ... smelling like gun powder ... stood up to lay blame as he shook off colored strips of thin paper streamers from his shirt & trousers. The startled '**Photographer**' grabbed their toppling camera, accidently pressing the flash button which distressed the '**Quiet**' person, causing her to pass wind. She was so embarrassed ... she blushed.

CLUE 13

As the room was filled with the foul odour, one person raced out the door, and another made a bee-line to open the window. Everyone else held their noses and moaned. One person just sat there and laughed.

QUESTIONS

Where was each person seated? *[Review all clues]*

How did the mysterious bomb scare happen? *[Review all clues]*

Who was involved in the mysterious bomb scare? *[Review all clues]*

Who was & where was the photographer? *[Review all clues]*

Who left the room? *[Review all clues]*

Who opened the window? *[Review all clues]*

Who left the room? *[Review all clues]*

Who opened the window? *[Review all clues]*

Who sat at the end and laughed? *[Review all clues]*

ONCE YOU HAVE REVIEWED ALL YOUR CLUES, THEN YOU CAN CHECK OUT THE SOLUTION / ANSWER AT THE BACK OF THE BOOK

Mini-World Mysteries
Chapter #2

"SCARECROW IN THE VEGIE PATCH MYSTERY"

- Your task is Your task is to successfully locate the correct position of the vegetables planted in the vegie patch.
- Also solve the mystery of where the **'SCARECROW'**, **'RAKE'** **'COMPOST'** & **'SPRINKLER'** are all located.
- READ through each clue *separately* & *carefully* e.g.

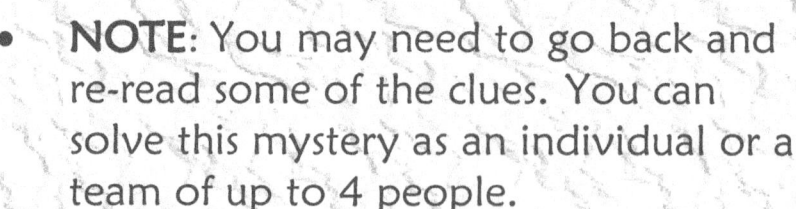

- **NOTE:** You may need to go back and re-read some of the clues. You can solve this mystery as an individual or a team of up to 4 people.

MINI WORLD MYSTERIES

TEMPLATE #2

"SCARECROW IN THE VEGIE PATCH MYSTERY"

Before you can solve this mystery, you will need to use the template provided.

On pages 20-22 you will find your B & W template for this **MINI WORLD MYSTERY**.

The pages can be photocopied or traced then cut out. Use white card, otherwise laminate your paper for durability.

You can also color them to brighten up the activity if you like.

Perhaps store your cut-outs in an envelope for re-use with friends or family.

Once your cut out template is prepared, you will be ready to begin solving this mystery which starts on page 23.

You will be given the explanation, scenario, clues and solutions.

If you are playing this activity as a group, nominate one person to be the narrator/reader/adjudicator.

Print/trace/copy these next 3 pages

Color these

Cut these out

MINI WORLD MYSTERIES

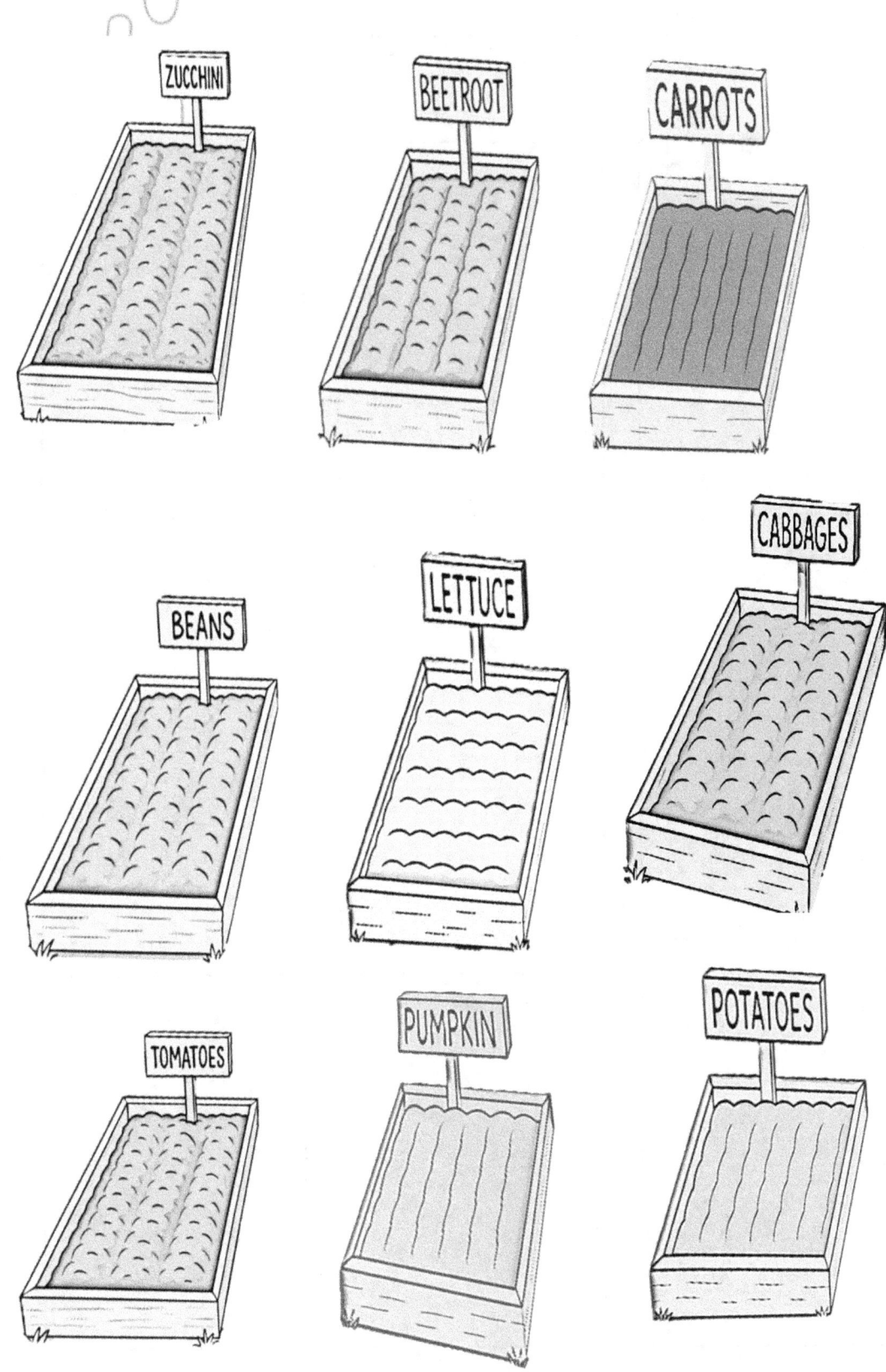

SCARECROW VEGIE PATCH MYSTERY

CLUES

CLUE 1: The gardener wanted the beans to be located near the fence … so they'd have something climb up.

CLUE 2: The lettuces should be planted near the **SPRINKLER** … and the zucchini, BUT should be kept away from the beans!

CLUE 3: The compost heap was positioned behind the fence, near the beetroot. The **SCARECROW** was to be nowhere near the compost heap. The gardener did not want to scare the worms!

CLUE 4: For some strange reason the gardener believed that the tomatoes would grow better when planted next to the carrots.

CLUE 5: The potatoes were in-between the beans and beetroot ... BUT not near the cabbages or the **SPRINKLER**.

CLUE 6: The carrots should be *BEHIND* the lettuces ... AND in-front of the beans.

CLUE 7: The pumpkin should be in-front of the beetroot ... AND next to the tomatoes.

CLUE 8: The **SPRINKLER** is best suited to being placed close to the cabbages and zucchini ... which need a lot of water.

MINI WORLD MYSTERIES

CLUE 9
Beetroot should be planted near the fence ... AND next to the potatoes.

CLUE 10
The zucchinis are to be planted in-front of the tomatoes ... AND in-between the lettuces and cabbages

CLUE 11
The cabbages should not be near the carrots OR the potatoes.

CLUE 12
The **SCARECROW** needed to be positioned in-between the tomatoes AND the beans, so that it didn't get too wet. Apparently, his umbrella blew away on the last windy day!

SCARECROW VEGIE PATCH MYSTERY

The **GARDINER'S** phone rang just when he'd picked up the rake. She was startled and dropped the rake, leaving it in a dangerous position at the end of the fence furthest from the cabbages. That was the end of gardening for the day!

QUESTIONS

Where were each of the vegetables planted? *[Review all clues]*

Where was the **FENCE** positioned? *[Review all clues]*

Where was the **COMPOST** positioned? *[Review all clues]*

Where was the **SPRINKLER** positioned? *[Review all clues]*

Where was the **SCARECROW** positioned? *[Review all clues]*

Where was the **RAKE** positioned? *[Review all clues]*

ONCE YOU HAVE REVIEWED ALL YOUR CLUES, THEN YOU CAN CHECK OUT THE *'SOLUTIONS FILE'* AT THE BACK OF THE BOOK

Mini-World Mysteries
Chapter #3

"A Walk in the Park Mystery"

- Your task is to correctly position the flowers in the park, in relation to other elements.
- Also find out where the pond, path and park bench are positioned, and in which direction the dog & owner were walking.
- The real mystery has to do with the ball and the bone.
- READ through each clue **separately** & **carefully** e.g. 🔑 CLUE 1

- **NOTE**: You may need to go back and re-read some of the clues. You can solve this mystery as an individual or a team of up to four people.

MINI WORLD MYSTERIES

TEMPLATE #3

'A WALK IN THE PARK MYSTERY'

On Over the next few pages you will find your B & W template for this **MINI WORLD MYSTERY**.

The pages can be photocopied or traced then cut out. Use white card, otherwise laminate your paper for durability.

You can also color them to brighten up the activity if you like.

Perhaps store your cut-outs in an envelope for re-use with friends or family.

Once your cut out template is prepared, you will be ready to begin solving this mystery which starts on page 33.

You will be given the explanation, scenario, clues and solutions.

If you are playing this activity as a group, nominate one person to be the narrator/reader/adjudicator.

A WALK IN THE PARK MYSTERY

Print/trace/copy these next 3 pages

Color these

Cut these out

Pond

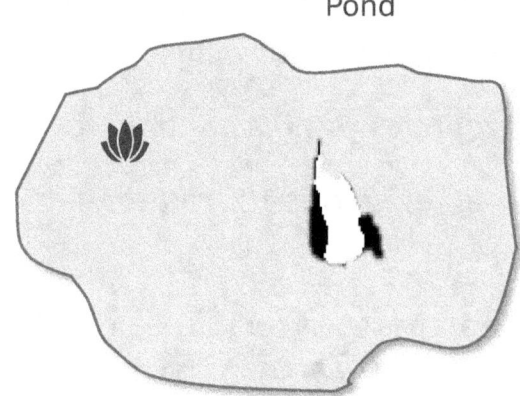

White flowers

Orange flowers

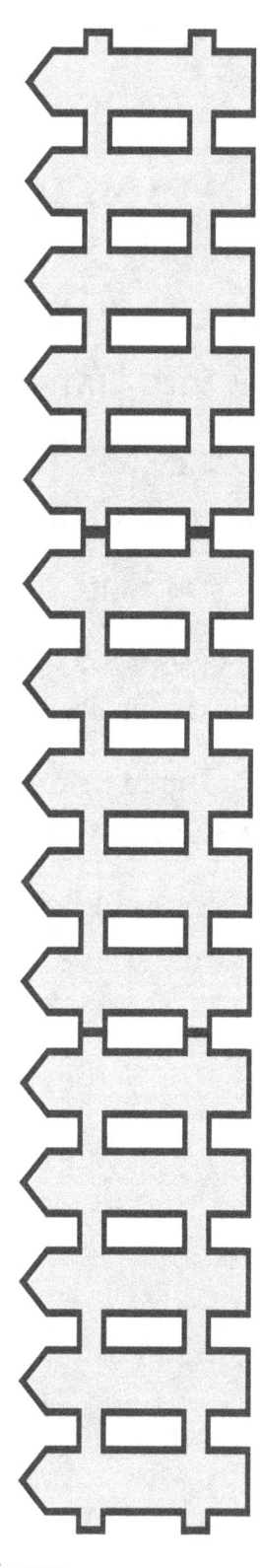

Fence

MINI WORLD MYSTERIES

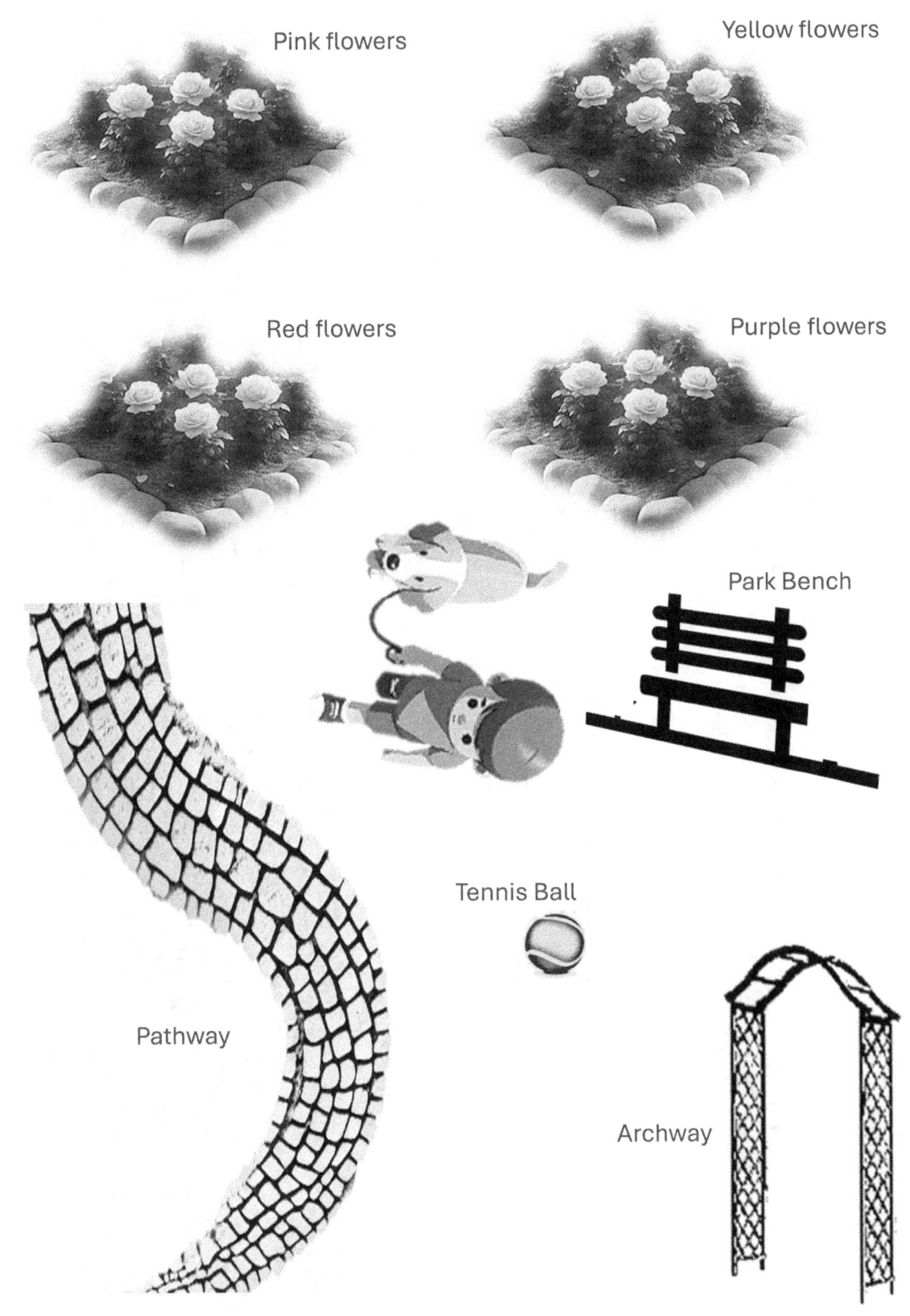

A WALK IN THE PARK MYSTERY

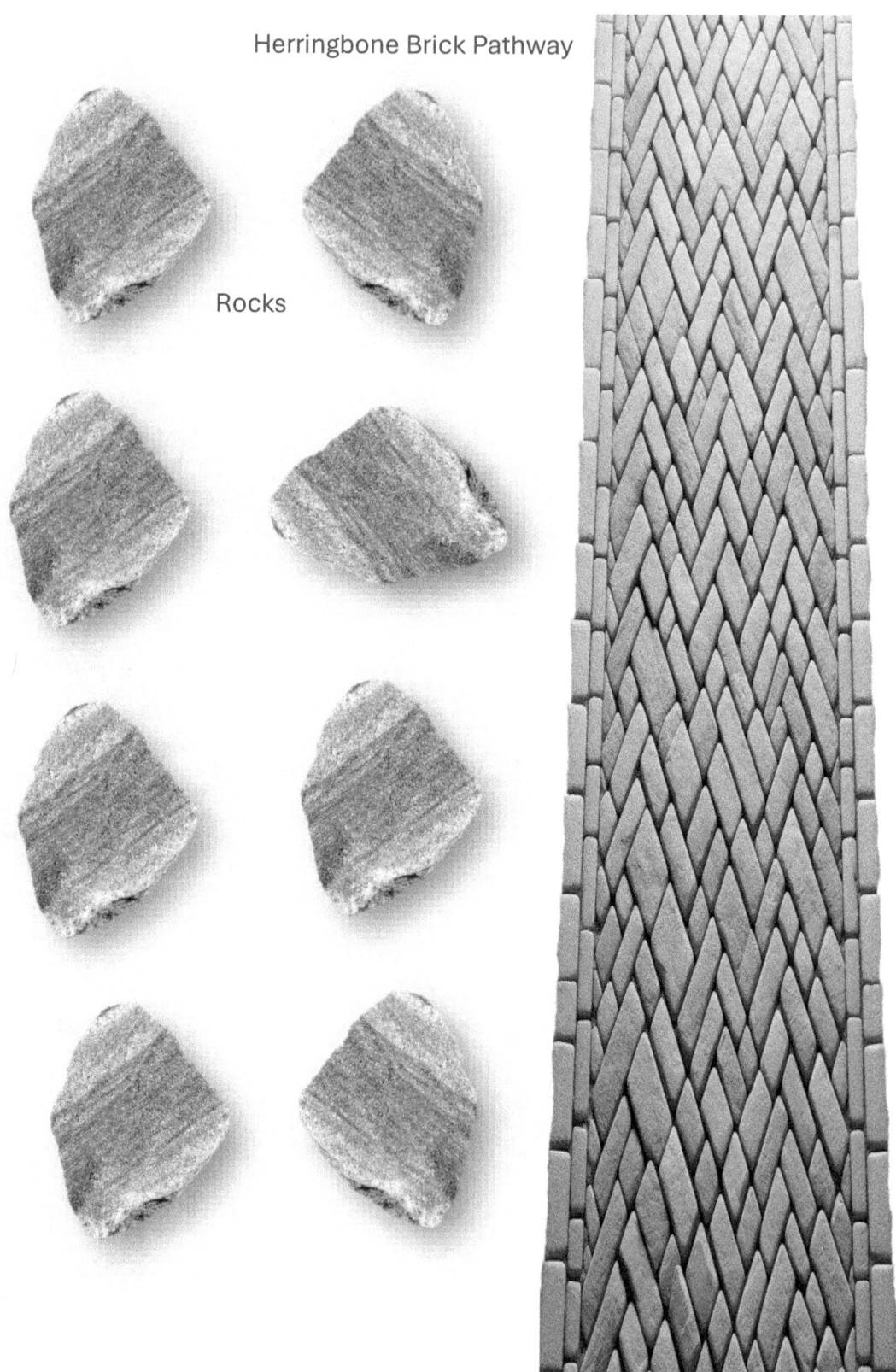

Herringbone Brick Pathway

Rocks

CLUES

- The pathway is in-between the white flowers and orange flowers.
- The park bench is not near the pink flowers.
- The pathway has yellow flowers at one end.
- The gated archway is not near the pond.

- The outside of the fence faces north ... where the rocks are.
- The pond is not near the park bench.
- The orange flowers are not situated near the pond, but next to the yellow flowers.

- The red flowers are to the right of the pond, but they are not opposite the pink flowers.
- The white flowers are not near the pink flowers but closest to the park bench.
- The yellow and purple flowers are situated south of the pathway, but at opposite ends.

A WALK IN THE PARK MYSTERY

CLUE 4
- The orange flowers are closest to the outside [*herringbone*] path on the south edge of the scene.
- The red & pink flowers are nearest to the pond.
- The park bench is at the east end of the park near the fence.

CLUE 5
- The pond is located towards the west end of the park but not too close to the fence.
- The pink flowers are furthest from the park bench.
- As a dog named **SHERLAC** & his owner walked through the gated archway and down the cobblestone path, they had white flowers to their right and purple flowers on their left.

CLUE 6
- Together, the young lad and his Pug dog **SHERLAC** form an unstoppable detective duo, roaming their quiet little town and tackling puzzles big and small. Whether it's finding a missing item, uncovering secrets, or outsmarting mischievous troublemakers, their partnership is built on trust, cleverness, and a shared sense of adventure.
- As they stepped off the path, the owner released his dog and threw his ball towards the pond.
- **SHERLAC** barked and frightened a duck which was foraging under the red flowers on the right.
- The duck flew off as the dog searched for the ball.
- The dog's name is an anagram of his owner's name.

7 QUESTIONS

- Where did the ball end up?
- Where did the duck fly to? What did it do?
- What direction were the dog & owner walking?
- What is the dog owner's name?
- Where was the bone?

ONCE YOU HAVE REVIEWED ALL YOUR CLUES, THEN YOU CAN CHECK OUT THE *'SOLUTIONS FILE'* AT THE BACK OF THE BOOK

36

Mini-World Mysteries

Chapter #4

"K-9 Capers Mystery"

- Your task will be to solve this multi-layered mystery. This mystery has two phases. The first one is on the **BLACK BOARD** ... the other one is on the **WHITE BOARD**.
- **NOTE:** The *BLACK PHASE* needs to be solved first.
- You can solve this mystery as an individual or a team of up to four people.
- READ through each numbered clue *separately* & *carefully* e.g.

K-9 CAPERS MYSTERY

K-9 CAPERS MYSTERY TEMPLATE

Over the next seven pages can be photocopied or traced then cut out. Use white card, otherwise laminate your paper for durability.

You can also color them to brighten up the activity if you like.

Perhaps store your cut-outs in an envelope for re-use with friends or family.

Once your cut out template is prepared, you will be ready to begin solving this mystery which starts on page 47.

You will be given the explanation, scenario, clues and solutions. The solutions for this mystery will require a mirror.

If you are playing this activity as a group, nominate one person to be the narrator/reader/adjudicator.

Print/trace/copy the next 7 pages

Color these

Cut these out

TABLE TALK MYSTERY — MINI WORLD MYSTERIES

K-9 CAPERS MYSTERY

MINI WORLD MYSTERIES

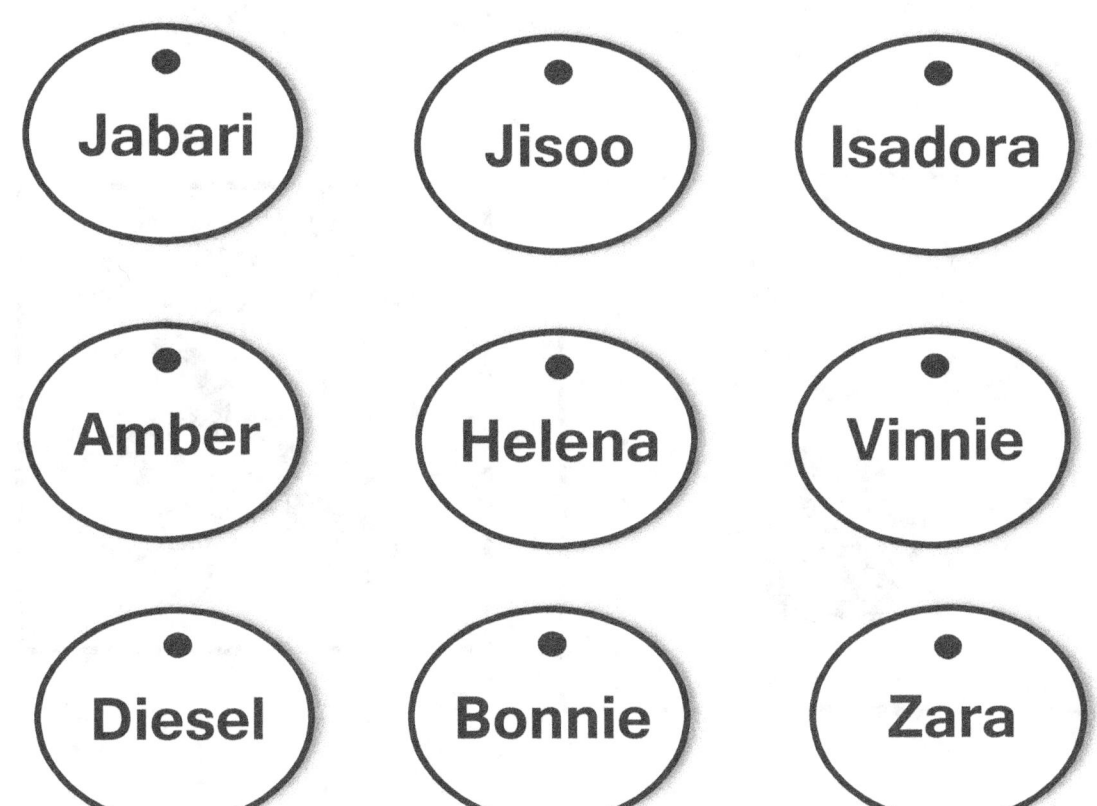

FOR THE WHITE BOARD LAYOUT, YOU CAN POSITION THE VARIOUS VENUES ANYWHERE YOU CHOOSE.

MINI WORLD MYSTERIES

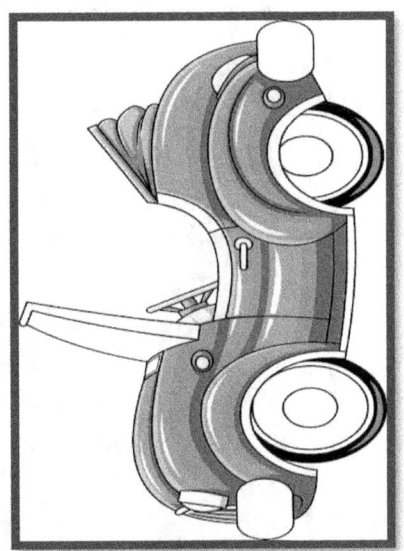

K-9 CAPERS MYSTERY

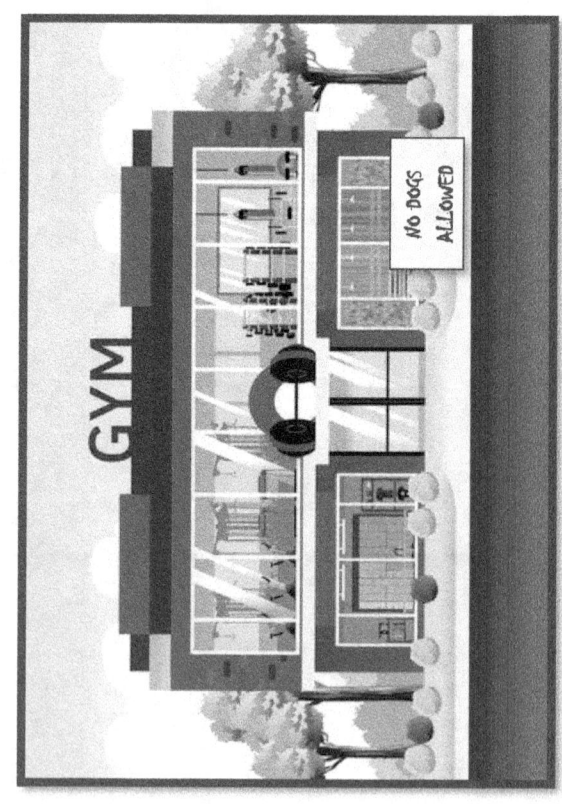

MINI WORLD MYSTERIES

BLACK SIDE — CLUES

BLACK SIDE — TASK #1

CLUE 1
- Match each dog with a name. MOST names are cryptic ... not as they might appear! Place each dog's name tag next to the corresponding dog.
- The Toy Poodle looks yummy and Roxie is basically one color.
- The tallest dog does not have the longest name ... and the smallest dog does not have the cutest name.
- Roxie & Shadow are opposite colors and Muffin's coat is quite stylish.
- The Pug snorts a lot and Rambo is black & light brown.

CLUE 2
- Check your answers in the envelope labelled **'DOG'S NAMES'** at the back of the book.
- If you correctly matched them all ... score your team **10 points**.
- Otherwise simply subtract *from 10* the ones you got wrong. Make sure all the names are correct before moving onto TASK TWO.

BLACK SIDE — TASK #2

- Match each **PERSON-CHARACTER** with a name.
- Place each character's name tag net to the corresponding person.
- Jabari is a boy's name and Jisoo is female.
- Vinnie likes hiking … Amber is a social chatterbox.
- Isadora is flamboyant … both Jabari and Bonnie are the youngest.
- Jisoo wears bright sunnies and Helena never wears jeans.

- Check your answers in the envelope labelled **'PEOPLE'S NAMES'** at the back of the book.
- Score your team 10 … if you correctly matched them all.
- Otherwise simply subtract the ones you got wrong from 10. Make sure all the names are correct before moving onto **TASK THREE**.
- **TALLY YOUR task #1 & #2 SCORES out of 20.**

MINI WORLD MYSTERIES

BLACK SIDE — TASK #3

5 CLUE
- Match each DOG with their OWNER.
- Shadow's coat is the same color as his owner's shorts.
- Muffin's owner likes to tizzy things up a bit.
- Bounce is an active dog who likes long walks.
- Pee Wee's owner is fit, but does not have tattoos.
- Jisoo has a sweet tooth.
- Shadow's owner looks tough but is a real softy at heart.

6 CLUE
- Check your answers in the envelope labelled **'DOGS & OWNERS'** at the back of the book.
- Score your team 10 ... if you correctly matched them all.
- Otherwise simply subtract the ones you got wrong from 10. Make sure all the names are correct before moving onto TASK FOUR.
- **TALLY YOUR SCORES out of 30.**

END OF PHASE ONE — BLACK SIDE

- Check your SCORES out of 30. If you scored a perfect score then add a bonus 10. [A perfect score now equals 40!]
- If you did not score a perfect score but were above 30, then add a bonus 5. Between 20 & 30 add a bonus 2 points.
- You are now ready to begin **PHASE TWO**. Remove all the characters & dogs from the BLACK SIDE and turn the board over.
- *IT'S YOUR CHOICE TO STOP HERE OR CONTINUE ... YOU CAN TAKE A BREAK IF YOU NEED TO.*
- If you decide to continue ... move all the dogs and owners off the edge of the WHITE BOARD SIDE
- You will not need to use the dog collars in this phase. Place them in a safe place.
- READ through each clue *separately* & *carefully.*

MINI WORLD MYSTERIES

WHITE SIDE – CLUES

WHITE SIDE — TASK #1

- Check out all the possibilities of places for dogs and owners to be found
- WALKING TRACK ... DOG FRIENDLY PARK ... BACKYARD ... SOFA ... VETENARY ... GYMNASIUM ... CAR RIDE ... TRAINING SCHOOL ... DOG GROOMERS ... PET STORE ... DOG FRIENDLY BEACH
- Think about each dog & their owner's characteristics and interests.

Your sleuthing task is to place each paired dog & owner where you think they might be found.

- Vinnie likes hiking.
- Flamboyant Isadora trained as a hairdresser.
- Social chatterbox Amber was always looking for ways to connect with other dog owners.
- Jisoo had light-sensitive eyes and therefore chose to walk only before sunrise or after sunset.

CLUE 3

- Zara's dog Pee Wee loved the fresh air and because he was so big and strong, she had to find ways to get him out and about but restrict his movements. He did not like getting wet.
- Shadow's owner Deisel was a compulsive fitness trainer.
- Roxie was an active dog and needed daily walks. He also needed to be housed securely when Jabari was at school.

CLUE 4

- Bonnie was always on the lookout for new toys for her dog, but more importantly she found out that Pugs needed constant physical check-ups.
- Helen began to realise that although they were very cute looking — King Charles Cavaliers were so strong-willed.

MINI WORLD MYSTERIES

5 QUESTIONS

- Who would you expect to find going for all day walks?
- Who would you expect to find quite often at home on the sofa?
- Who would you expect to find at the K-9 Clippers?
- Which dogs would you *NOT* expect to find at the beach?
- Which dog was the loneliest dog?
- Which dog went to the park most days?

6 QUESTIONS

- Who would you expect to find at the obedience training?
- Where would you expect to find Bonnie & Snorty on the weekends?
- Which dog would you expect to spend more time in a restricted environment?
- Which dog would you expect to most likely try to escape and try to find their owner?

QUESTIONS

- Which dog was pulled over by the police for not wearing a seatbelt?
- Which dog was picked up by the Dog-Pound for loitering outside the gym?
- Which dog spent most time at the veterinary clinic?
- Which dogs had the best chance to meet at the park?

CHECK YOUR ANSWERS IN THE ENVELOPES at the BACK of the BOOK

Mini-World Mysteries
Chapter #5

"TEDDY BEARS' PICNIC MISHAPS MYSTERY"

- Your task is to solve the mystery surrounding the mishaps of the colored Teddy Bears in relation to other elements in the story.
- This mystery has a lot to do with the balloons, bows, baskets and of course ... the bears.
- You can solve this mystery as an individual or a team of up to four people.
- READ through each numbered clue *separately* & *carefully* e.g.

MINI WORLD MYSTERIES

TEMPLATE #5

'TEDDY BEARS' PICNIC MISHAPS MYSTERY'

Over the next five pages you will find your B & W template for this **MINI WORLD MYSTERY**.

The pages can be photocopied or traced then cut out. Use white card, otherwise laminate your paper for durability.

You can also color them to brighten up the activity if you like.

Perhaps store your cut-outs in an envelope for re-use with friends or family.

Once your cut out template is prepared, you will be ready to begin solving this mystery which starts on page 63.

You will be given the explanation, scenario, clues and solutions.

If you are playing this activity as a group, nominate one person to be the narrator/reader/adjudicator.

Print/trace/copy the next 5 pages

Color these

Cut these out

TEDDY BEAR'S PICNIC MYSTERY

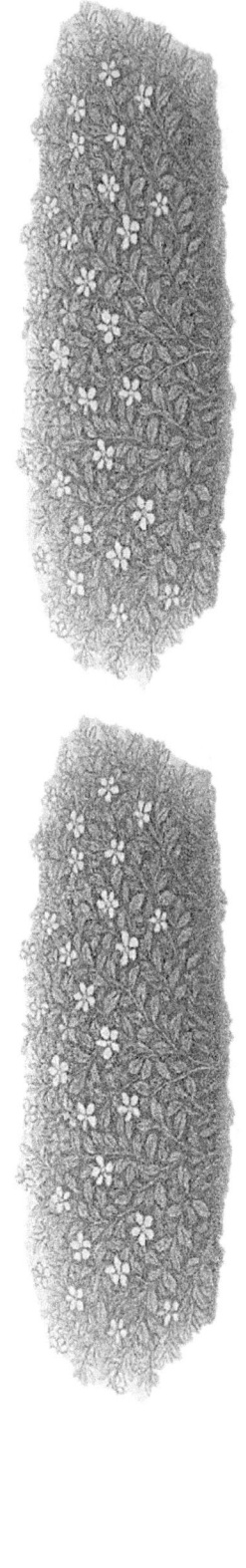

MINI WORLD MYSTERIES

TEDDY BEAR'S PICNIC MYSTERY

TEDDY BEAR COLORS:
* MAUVE
*RED
* YELLOW

RIBBON BOW COLORS:
YELLOW / RED / BLUE
GREEN / ORANGE
MAUVE / WHITE / PINK

BALLOON COLORS:
YELLOW / RED
BLUE / GREEN
ORANGE

TEDDY BEAR COLORS: ~~MAUVE~~ / ~~YELLOW~~ / ~~RED~~ / BLUE / ORANGE / PINK / WHITE
**BROWN with one small patch of *GREEN*

MINI WORLD MYSTERIES

PLAN OF THE TEDDY BEARS' PICNIC

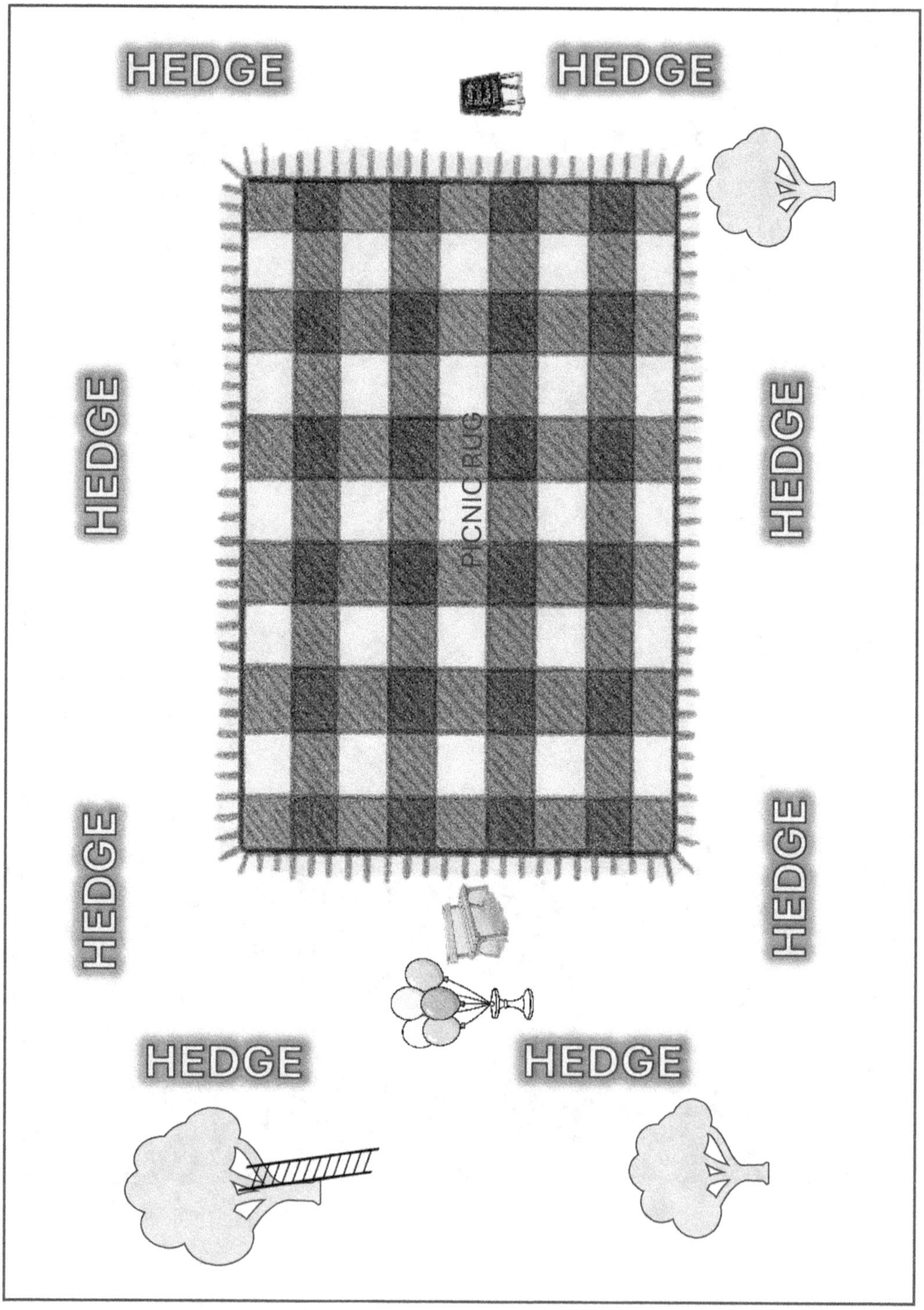

MINI WORLD MYSTERIES

Setting the Scene

The picnic takes place in a sun dappled clearing, featuring:

- A large picnic rug positioned in a park surrounded by 8 hedges.
- There are 3 trees, with the tallest having a ladder leaning against it.
- A wooden sign reading: "Teddy Bears' Picnic Today".
- A park bench.
- A bunch of five helium balloons, as three of them have disappeared.
- Eight different colored TEDDY BEARS
- Each bear has brought a picnic basket marked with a colored ribbon matching the color of their fur.
- The baskets contained different treats: Bread, Candy, Honey, Bananas & Grapes, Apples & Pears, Triangular Sandwiches, Full-slice Sandwiches and Easter Eggs.

CLUES

- After all the bears had arrived, and greeted each other, they set their baskets down. Their baskets were full of goodies they had prepared. They each placed their baskets in their chosen place on the large picnic blanket.
- The plan was to play first — then eat later.
- The bear they all called 'QUEENY' gathered everyone together and declared that they should all play a game of 'HIDE and SEEK'.

READ through each clue *separately* & *carefully*.

- For the sake of orientation, the sign reading: "Teddy Bears' Picnic Today" is located at the north entrance to the park.
- During the lively game of 'HIDE and SEEK', someone switched all the ribbons on the baskets. Now, every basket has the wrong ribbon — leading to confusion and suspicion among the bears.
- Someone released three of the balloons, and there also appears to be an intruder ... but that's just the beginning ... as someone also seems to have gone missing!

MINI WORLD MYSTERIES

- At the start of the 'HIDE and SEEK' game, Blue Bear was chosen by all the others to go '*it*'. He reluctantly agreed but was **not** happy.

- Blue Bear and Green Bear were best buddies and had planned to hide together, but now they not able to ... so Green Bear decided to venture beyond the boundaries of the park to hide, and unfortunately he had fallen into a muddy patch.

- 'Bell-Boy' Bear had been instructed to sound his bell to signal the start of the game. And then he was ordered ahead of time by 'Queeny' to ring his bell again after 5 minutes, to let everyone know that they had 5 minutes left.

- When the second bell rang out, as everyone scrambled to find their new hiding spaces ... someone decided it was the ideal time to have a bit of fun, and quickly rearranged all the ribbons on the picnic baskets as a joke.

- Amid the scrambling chaos, someone accidentally tripped over the balloon stand in their quest to find a new hiding place accidently releasing three of the balloons.

CLUE 5

- When the final bell rang out to signal the end of the 'HIDE and SEEK' game, everyone came back to the picnic area excitedly laughing as none of them were 'found' by the Blue Bear ... but they were all in for big surprise ... all except for Blue Bear and his muddy buddy, who just went and sat down.
- One of them sat on the park bench and the other on the picnic blanket next to their basket of goodies.

CLUE 6

- As the Teddy Bears all gathered and sharing about their hiding spots, they were stopped in their tracks as they noticed there was a brown bear sitting on the picnic blanket. Who was this strange looking, smelly bear and where was Green Bear?
- Then there were screams of shock all over the picnic area as one-by-one they each discovered that they had the wrong basket of goodies.
- At first they each started blaming one another for stealing their basket, but then as they realised the ribbons had been switched and that someone had done it to all of the baskets and ribbons. All except for one!

CLUE 7

- All the other bears immediately turned on the Brown Bear accusing him on switching the ribbons simply because he looked like an intruder. As the Brown Bear stood up to speak someone noticed that he sounded just like Green Bear, and then someone else noticed a green patch of fur on his back.
- Everyone laughed hysterically as he shared how he'd fallen into the mud patch.
- 'Queeny' then ordered that they all split up and search for clues as to what had happened and who the culprit was.
- 'Bell Boy' Bear was ordered by 'Queeny' to accompany her, so that she could tell him when to ring the bell for everyone to regroup after a few minutes.

CLUE 8

- The bears spread out in pairs searching for clues:
    - Yellow & Mauve searched the trees.
    - Red & Pink searched the hedges.
    - Orange & White searched around the park bench and balloons.
    - Blue & Green didn't really go anywhere at all.
- Here's what they discovered:
    - Red fur near the ladder tree and a Band-Aide wrapper nearby.
    - A piece of blue ribbon stuck in one of the hedges near the park bench.
    - Muddy footprints on the picnic blanket.

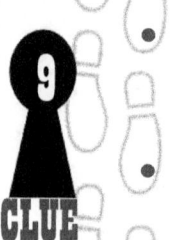

CLUE 9

- The bear who brought triangle sandwiches somehow had hurt their coccyx and so needed to sit on a soft cushion.
- The bossy bear — as well as the bear who had scraped their paw — both brought fruit.
- Blue Bear and Pink Bear both had a sweet tooth. Blue Bear was partial to licorice, while Pink Bear liked chocolate.
- The bell-ringing bear also had a sweet tooth in the form of a natural product.
- Large white bread sandwiches matched the color of the bear with this basket.
- And the biggest surprise of all was that the muddy bear ended up matching the color of goodies in their basket perfectly.

QUESTIONS

- Who switched the ribbons? Why?
- Match each basket with the correct ribbon (SIMPLY REMOVE AND RE-STICK with blue-tac)
- Match each basket with the correct colored Teddy Bear.
- What color was 'QUEENY'?
- Which bear scraped their leg/paw climbing the tree? How do you know?
- How come there was a piece of blue ribbon found in the hedge?
- Which bear came away from the picnic angry because everything was ruined?
- Which bear's basket ribbon was not switched at all? Why?
- At the end of it all, which bear was sitting on the park bench?
- Which three Teddy Bears went home without a balloon?
- Who wrote the *sign*: "Teddy Bears' Picnic"?
- Who wrote the *song*: "Teddy Bears' Picnic"?

CHECK YOUR ANSWERS IN THE ENVELOPES at the BACK of the BOOK

Mini-World Mysteries

Chapter #6

"The Mystery of King Azurepaw's Secret Garden"

- Your task will be to solve this multi-layered mystery.
- Use pen & paper to *record your findings* (if required).
- All will be revealed in the end!
- You can solve this mystery as an individual or a team of up to four people.
- READ through each numbered clue *separately* & *carefully* e.g.

MINI WORLD MYSTERIES

TEMPLATE #6

"THE MYSTERY OF KING AZUREPAW'S SECRET GARDEN"

Over the next two pages you will find your B & W template for this **MINI WORLD MYSTERY**.

The pages can be photocopied or traced then cut out. Use white card, otherwise laminate your paper for durability.

You can also color them to brighten up the activity if you like.

Perhaps store your cut-outs in an envelope for re-use with friends or family.

Once your cut out template is prepared, you will be ready to begin solving this mystery which starts on page 76.

You will be given the explanation, scenario, clues and solutions.

If you are playing this activity as a group, nominate one person to be the narrator/reader/adjudicator.

MYSTERY OF KING AZUREPAW'S GARDEN

Print/trace/copy the next 2 pages

Color these

Cut these out

King Azurepaw's Secret Garden Basic Lay Out

MINI WORLD MYSTERIES

Setting the Scene

Beyond the reach of roads lies a hidden garden which no-one may enter without the King's permission. In this secret garden, the trees whisper. The brook hums lullabies. And its King is a soft, round blue bear named Azurepaw.

He wears a golden crown and a bow-tie, but he has no robe. With quiet dignity, he rules his world. Each dawn, he walks the mossy paths, taps the wishing well with his favourite stick, and listens to the stillness of the whispers and babbling brook.

Now and then, a child — or even a pig — peeks through a hole in the wall, hoping to catch a glimpse of the King's secret garden, or even the King himself.

Inside, mysteries await to be uncovered. Many have tried but few have succeeded. Will you? How can you get in?

CLUES

- The King had some of his servants plant this miniature walled-garden, where he could relax on his cane chair, sip from his drink bottle, and look out over it.
- The problem being ... he is way too big to walk through it, without causing damage.
- And yet he does manage to walk through his secret garden every day, without trampling the trees and bridge under his big blue paws. How does he do it? What / where was his secret?

- One day as the King was walking through the garden he realised that he'd lost his crown jewel.
- What had happened to it? Was it stolen? If so by whom?
- Where could it be? How might he get it back?

- Outside the locked gates there is a bell-post. People who pass by, love to ring the bell — not just for the sound but also to see if the king would invite them in. It should be positioned to the right of the padlocked gates. **[PLACE THE BELL-POST IN POSITION]**

MYSTERY OF KING AZUREPAW'S GARDEN

- If only people knew the password they would be invited into the secret garden.
- Written on the handle of the Bell-post rope are clues for the password to enter the secret garden.
- The password contains 3 syllables. What is the password? Two visible clues are on the outside of the wall and also atop the wall of his castle.

- The King loved to sit under the shade of a large tree on his left. What was the color of the tree? These clues will help.
  - **Yellow** is bright and cheerful, and liveliness.
  - **Pink** carries the essence of calm, kindness, and quiet joy. It's a color that whispers rather than shouts. It invites stillness, listening, and the quiet work of tending dreams.
  - **Red** is bold—fiery, commanding, and passionate. King Azurepaw is composed and understated.
- **POSITION THE TREE IN PLACE**

MINI WORLD MYSTERIES

- The large red tree is closest to the brook.
- On the other side of the pathway are 4 smaller trees.
- The hammock hangs between the two green trees. It is not near the side table, nor is it close to the brook.
- The small yellow tree is closest to the King's side table.
- **POSITION THESE ITEMS IN PLACE**

- The wishing-well is situated in between the pathway and the other two large trees.
- The bridge does not cross the pathway. It crosses the brook in a direct line with the pathway and the King.
- The King is right handed, so where would his side table be placed?
- **POSITION THESE ITEMS IN PLACE**

- The WEATHERVANE indicates the direction of the slight breeze.
- The pathway from the King to the brook is positioned west-to-east.
- This should help you figure out which direction the breeze is blowing.

MYSTERY OF KING AZUREPAW'S GARDEN

9 CLUE

- The King loves to sail his little yacht on the gently flowing brook which flows from the mountains in the north towards the sea in the south.
- From where the yacht is on the water, is it travelling towards the bridge or away from the bridge?
- Using this information should help you figure out which direction the brook flows.

QUESTIONS

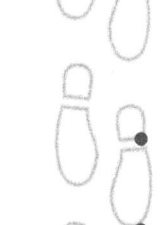
1 QUESTIONS

- How does the king manage to walk through his secret garden every day, without trampling the trees and bridge under his big blue paws? What / where is he secret?
- Written on the handle of the Bell-post rope are clues for the password to enter the secret garden. **[W-B]** The password consists of 2 words with 3 syllables.
  o The two visible clues on the outside of the wall and atop the wall of his castle.
  o What is the password?
- What color was the tree the King loved to sit under the shade of.
- What direction is the breeze blowing?
- Is the yacht moving towards or away from the bridge?

MINI WORLD MYSTERIES

QUESTIONS

- What happened to the CROWN JEWEL?
    - Was it stolen or misplaced?
- How might the King get it back?
- The clock *[not visible]* on the back of the courtyard wall showed 2.50 pm. The clock chimed a certain number of times every hour according to the time, then once on the half-hour. However, because the hands were stuck, the mystery was it was still showing the same time, when the King realised that the CROWN JEWEL was missing.
- The King had heard 8 chimes heard before realising the CROWN JEWEL was missing …
    - What was the time when the King actually realised that the CROWN JEWEL was missing?
    - What was the actual time when the CROWN JEWEL was stolen or went missing?
- Why were the clock hands stuck?

CHECK YOUR ANSWERS IN THE ENVELOPES at the BACK of the BOOK

Mini-World Mysteries

Chapter #7

"Hanging Out... On-Line Mystery"

- Your task will be to solve this multi-layered mystery.
- Use pen & paper to *record your findings* (if required).
- All will be revealed in the end!
- You can solve this mystery as an individual or a team of up to four people.
- READ through each numbered clue *separately* & *carefully* e.g.

TEMPLATE #7

"HANGING OUT ... ON-LINE MYSTERY"

Over the next two pages you will find your B & W template for this **MINI WORLD MYSTERY**.

The pages can be photocopied or traced then cut out. Use white card, otherwise laminate your paper for durability.

You can also color them to brighten up the activity if you like.

Perhaps store your cut-outs in an envelope for re-use with friends or family.

Once your cut out template is prepared, you will be ready to begin solving this mystery which starts on page 88.

You will be given the explanation, scenario, clues and solutions.

If you are playing this activity as a group, nominate one person to be the narrator/reader/adjudicator.

HANGING OUT ON-LINE MYSTERY

Print/trace/copy the next 2 pages

Color these

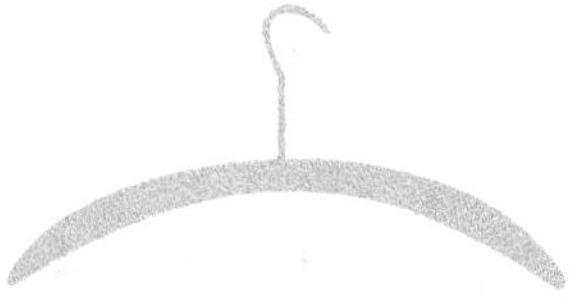

Cut these out

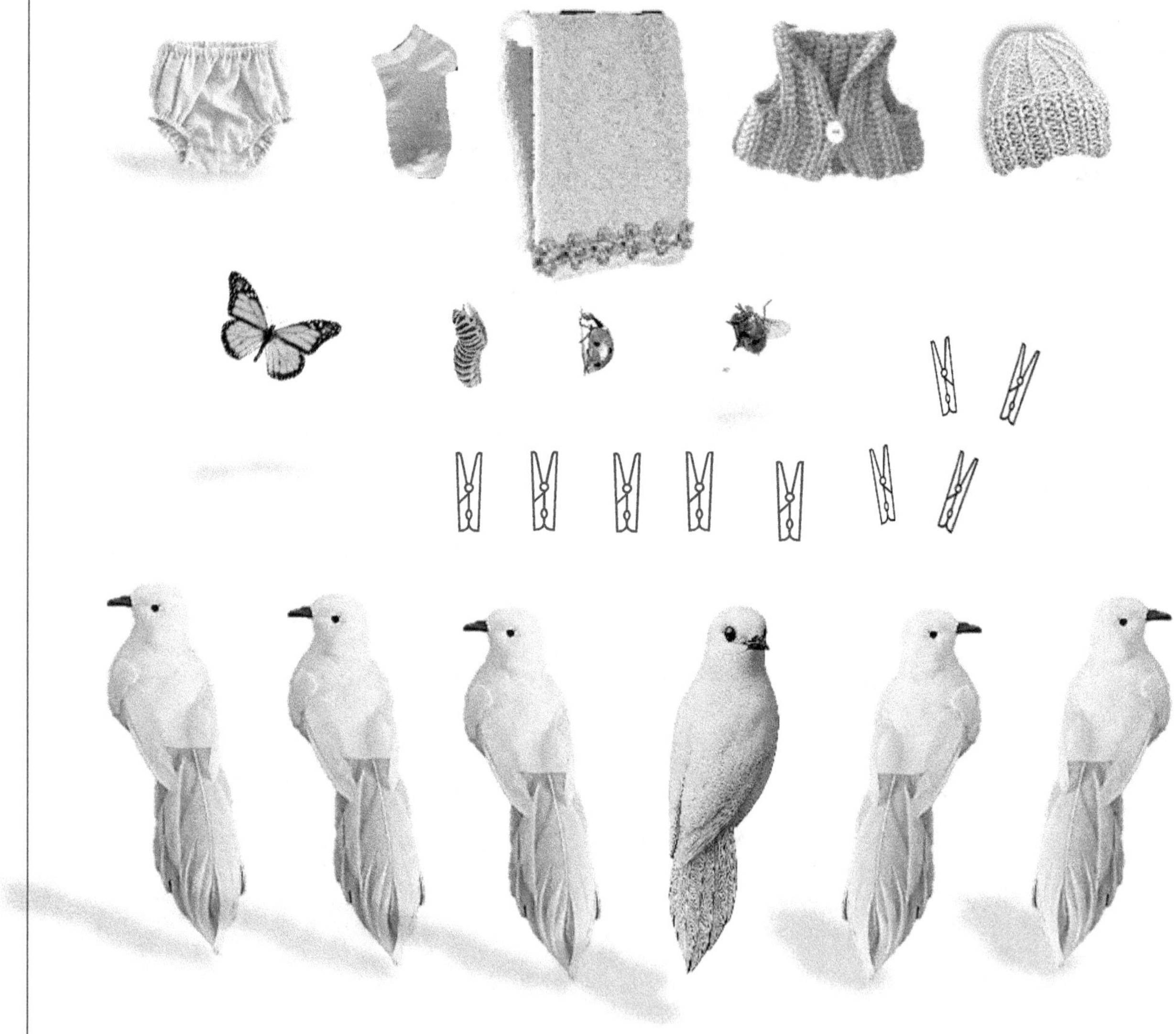

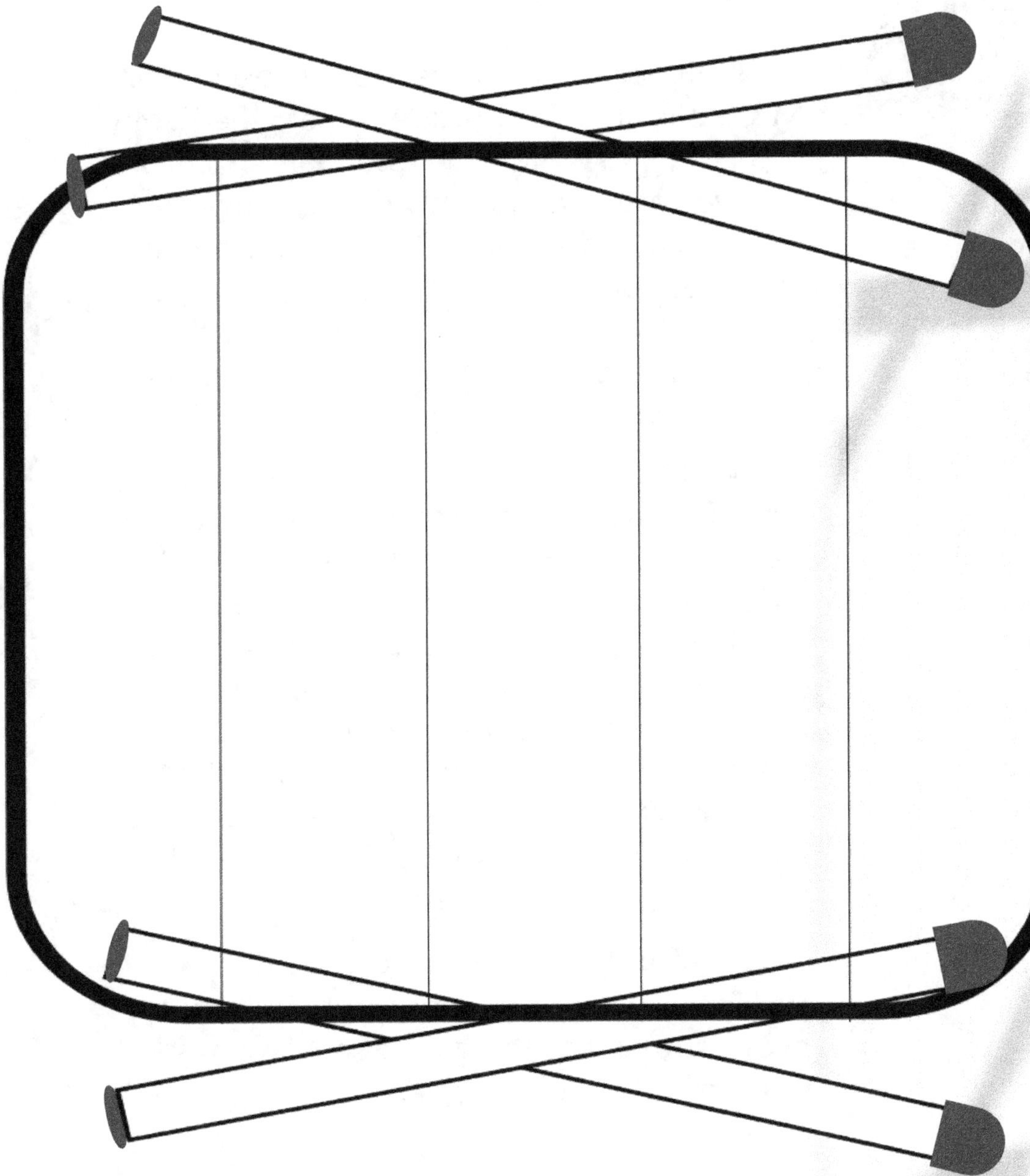

MINI WORLD MYSTERIES

87

Setting the Scene

It all began on a breezy afternoon when Miss Polly stepped outside to hang her Dolly's dainty laundry—just the essentials. There was a towel, a pair of socks, a knitted vest, bloomers, and a yellow beanie. She pegged them carefully along the four wires strung across her collapsable clothesline. But the strong breeze wasn't the only thing stirring up trouble.

Miss Polly went inside to make herself a cup of hot chocolate. Sometime later she peered out of her window. She was startled to find that the yellow beanie had fallen off the line onto the ground. She also noticed that the vest and bloomers had been *moved!* And to make things even more mysterious — there was a flamboyant flock of **six brightly colored birds** now sitting on the wires like a feathery lineup of suspects: Red, Green, Blue, Purple, Yellow, and Orange.

Each of the birds were perched suspiciously on clothesline — their innocent eyes betraying nothing. The scene was rich with mystery and intrigue.

Setting the Scene cont'd.

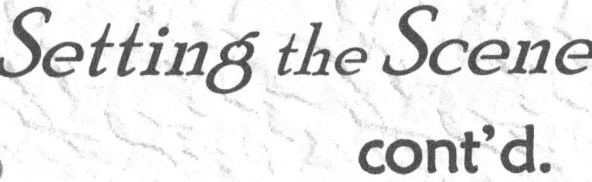

- The **bloomers**, once secure in the middle of the second line, were now pegged **on the front line**, held by **green and orange pegs**.
- The **vest**, no longer in its original spot on the front line, now dangled from the **second line**, clutched by **yellow and blue pegs**.
- Now only one **sock** sat oddly on the back line, held only by a single **plain peg**.
- The **towel**, once crisp and straight on the third line, now drooped by a **plain peg** on the front line.
- The **yellow beanie** which had hung on the back line, now lay silently beneath the clothesline frame.

None of the birds were talking, however four tiny creatures *might* have seen everything:

- A **blue butterfly** fluttered innocently on the top of the right inside leg—perhaps enjoying a 'bird's-eye view'!
- A **green caterpillar** slowly climbed the left inside leg, taking its time but seeing much.
- A **red ladybug** crawled up the right outside leg—nosey as ever.
- And a **black blowfly**, humming ominously, sat on the frame just behind the fourth line. Watchful. Perhaps even... menacing?

CLUES

- READ through each clue *separately* & *carefully*.
- The clues are intentionally *cryptic* ... but they are also *critical*.

"FRONT-LINE NEWS from BEHIND the SCENES"

☐ *RUBY THE RED BIRD:*

Perch Location : Front line centre.
Personality: Proud, bold, and very vocal.
Alibi: *"I never touch the clothes—I'm just here to sing!"*
Suspicion: She was seen eyeing the vest's moments just before it was moved... ... and now THE VEST is clipped with red and blue pegs, instead of two plain pegs.

"FRONT-LINE NEWS from BEHIND the SCENES"

☐ *GRACIE THE GREEN BIRD*

Perch Location: Right side, second front line.
Personality: Smart, sneaky, always planning something.
Alibi: *"I was watching the caterpillar crawl. Nature's just so fascinating!"*
Suspicion: Bloomers were moved... and now held by green and orange pegs right in front of her perch.

MINI WORLD MYSTERIES

"FRONT-LINE NEWS from BEHIND the SCENES"

☐ *BLUEBELL THE BLUE BIRD*

Perch Location: Second back line – in the centre facing away from Miss Polly's window.
Personality: Gentle, but always near the action.
Alibi: *"I stayed in my spot. I didn't fly an inch."*
Suspicion: The vest, once on the coat-hanger, is now held by two pegs — one of them blue. Could Bluebell have helped reposition it?

"FRONT-LINE NEWS from BEHIND the SCENES"

☐ *PENNY THE PURPLE BIRD*

Perch Location: Back left, furthest from Miss Polly's window.
Personality: Quiet and observant—always watching.
Alibi: *"I never move. I like to keep to myself."*
Suspicion: Had the best view of everything... perhaps the *puppet master* of the flock?

HANGING OUT ON-LINE MYSTERY

"FRONT-LINE NEWS from BEHIND the SCENES"

☐ SUNNY THE YELLOW BIRD

Perch Location: Back right.
Favourite Peg: Yellow.
Personality: Cheerful, but competitive.
Alibi: *"I was in a song battle with Ruby, didn't notice anything else."*
Suspicion: A yellow peg is now holding the towel.

"FRONT-LINE NEWS from BEHIND the SCENES"

☐ OLLIE THE ORANGE BIRD

Perch Location: Second front line. Behind Ruby to the left.
Personality: Nosy and playful, always meddling.
Alibi: *"I thought the towel needed fluffing!"*
Suspicion: Bloomers are now held by an orange peg and another of a different color. Ollie was not too far away.

MINI WORLD MYSTERIES

"FRONT-LINE NEWS from BEHIND the SCENES"

THE LINE WAS BUGGED!

 **CLUE 7**

 BONNIE THE BUTTERFLY

Perch: Atop the right inside leg.
Observation Point: The whole scene from above.
What She Saw: *"I saw feathers fly and bloomers float... but my lips are sealed."*
Clue: Saw something fall from the third line area. Maybe the beanie?

"FRONT-LINE NEWS from BEHIND the SCENES"

THE LINE WAS BUGGED!

 **CLUE 8**

🐛 **CLIVE THE CATERPILLAR**

Location: Crawling up the left inside leg.
Movement: Slow and low.
What He Saw: *"All I know is... that towel didn't always hang like that."*
Clue: Likely saw something shift near the front left.

"FRONT-LINE NEWS from BEHIND the SCENES"

THE LINE WAS BUGGED!

 LOLA THE LADYBUG

Location: Outside leg, right side.
Attitude: Busybody.
What She Saw: *"Someone knocked that beanie off. I felt the breeze."*
Clue: Was possibly closest to the yellow beanie before it fell.

"FRONT-LINE NEWS from BEHIND the SCENES"

THE LINE WAS BUGGED!

 BUZZ THE BLOWFLY

Location: Rear left arm of frame.
Attitude: Fed up with being told to '*Buzz Off!*'
Alibi: *"I just like the smell of clean laundry."*
Suspicion: Was *originally* close to the remaining sock being held by one plain peg. Did he loosen it?

"FINAL FORENSIC CLUES"

- No clothes were hanging on the third line. Yet Miss Polly hung them across all four lines.
- All the birds were chirping, but not all facing the same direction.
- Every creature was settled except for one.
- Every creature could fly except for one.
- All birds were facing the window except for one.
- □ Ollie & □ Gracie were on the same line as the vest, but at opposite ends.

"LAST CHANCE TO CHECK CLUES"

- Check where each item of clothing is now positioned.
- Check where each bird was sitting on the lines.
- Check which direction were they facing.
- Who moved the clothes? Was it all a frame-up or a playful activity gone too far?
- You will now be offered three **HYPOTHETICAL SOLUTIONS** to this *online* debacle.
- Which of these hypotheticals offers the best solution for you?

FINAL THOUGHTS

- **MASTERCLASS — ONE LAST CHALLENGE:** *Remove all the birds.*

Using your sleuthing prowess by working backwards ... try to figure out where each item of clothing was originally hung on the line by Miss Polly.

What is the most common letter used in the color of the birds? How many?

   o Answers ... see BACK OF THE BOOK

Thank you for *HANGING OUT ONLINE !*

Mini-World Mysteries
Chapter #8

"Mysterious Butterfly Frenzie @#54"

© Gary Lewis 1999/2025

- Your challenge will be to solve this multi-layered mystery.
- Along the way you will need to correctly position the flowerpots and butterflies, and other components along the garden fence of #54.
- The real mystery has to do with the cheese, the carrot, the rat, the frog, the cat & the bird.
- The butterflies and flowerpots are really only decoys.
- All will be revealed in the end!
- You can solve this mystery as an individual or a team of up to four people.
- READ through each numbered clue *separately* & *carefully* e.g.

1 CLUE

MINI WORLD MYSTERIES

TEMPLATE #8

"MYSTERIOUS BUTTERFLY FRENZIE @ #54"

Over the next few pages you will find your B & W template for this **MINI WORLD MYSTERY**.

The pages can be photocopied or traced then cut out. Use white card, otherwise laminate your paper for durability.

You can also color them to brighten up the activity if you like.

Perhaps store your cut-outs in an envelope for re-use with friends or family.

Once your cut out template is prepared, you will be ready to begin solving this mystery which starts on page 103.

You will be given the explanation, scenario, clues and solutions.

If you are playing this activity as a group, nominate one person to be the narrator/reader/adjudicator.

Print/trace/copy the next 3 pages

Color these

Cut these out

BUTTERFLY FRENZIE @#54

ORANGE & PINK

WHITE & PINK

PURPLE & YELLOW

RED & WHITE

MINI WORLD MYSTERIES

COLOR THE BUTTERFLIES AS YOU CHOOSE USING THE FOLLOWING COLORS:

GREEN & YELLOW x 1

BROWN & GREEN x 1

WHITISH x 2

ORANGE + YELLOW + BROWN x 2

PURPLE + BLUE + WHITE xx 1

REDDISH – WHITE x 1

GREEN + RED + WHITE x 1

YELLOW x 1

BUTTERFLY FRENZIE @#54

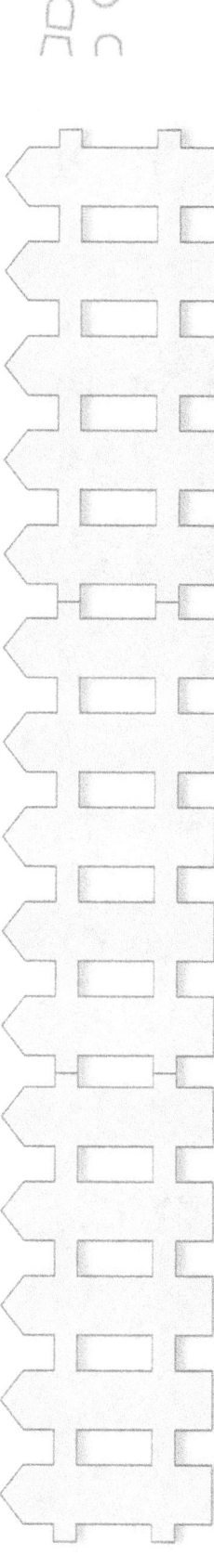
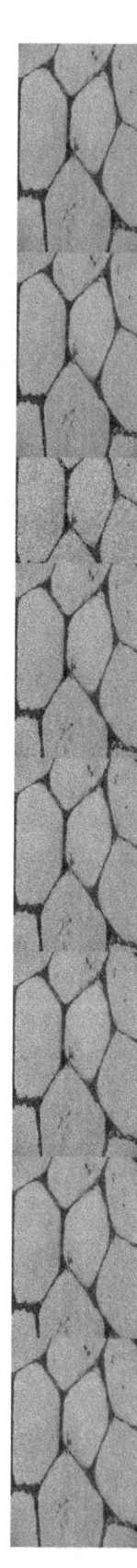

MINI WORLD MYSTERIES

Setting the Scene

A strong gust of wind terrorised all the creatures at #54. The cat frantically chased the bird, which chased the rat, which frightened the gnome and the frog.

The damselfly chased the bee which in turn upset all the butterflies. During this frenzied chaos, the flowerpots were all knocked over. After things had settled down, almost everything and everyone ended up totally out of place including the flowerpots.

A good Samaritan tried their best to reposition the flowerpots but they all ended up in the wrong spots.

Your sleuthing task is to **rearrange all the movable components** back to where they should be. And to **solve the mystery** surrounding the cheese, the carrot, the rat, the frog, the cat & the bird.

CLUES

- * READ through each clue *separately* & *carefully*.
- * They may be *cryptic* ... but they are also *critical*.
- #54 is on the outside of the garden fence.

- **On the inside of the garden fence**, the first pot on the left contained neither purple nor white flowers.
- The pot with pink & white flowers was in between the pots with red and purple flowers.

- The two pots containing white flowers were side by side.
- The orange and purple flowers were not near each other.
- The pot with red & white flowers should be directly to the right of where the bird is sitting.
- The purple flowers were not near the bird.
- The orange flowers were not near the cheese or gnome.

MINI WORLD MYSTERIES

CLUE 3

- Six of the eight butterflies were particularly attracted to colored flowers for camouflage.
- One butterfly was attracted to the front of the fence because of *its* color.
- The mushroom appreciated the shade from the green-red-white butterfly.
- The green-yellow butterfly was attracted to the same flowers as the whitish one.
- The butterfly which was mostly brown eventually landed on the 3-legged cat.

CLUE 4

- The two orange-colored butterflies were both attracted to the same pot, but only one landed.
- The two whitish butterflies tried to camouflage themselves.
- One butterfly did not have the proper landing gear and crashed-landed on the grass.
- The frog kept his distance from the gnome.
- The rat was having a feast hiding on the inside of the fence whilst looking out for predators.
- The purplish-blue butterfly was not bothered at all by the hovering bee.
- The carrot had been dug up just before the frenzy began.

5 QUESTIONS

- Who dug up the carrot?
- Who tried to steal the carrot? Why?
- Who stole the cheese ... why and when???
- Where did the butterfly without the proper landing gear end up?
- Where did the frog position himself and why?
- Who or what was the cat really after?
- If looks could be deceptive, then who was the real trouble maker? Why?
- Who was the good Samaritan who tried to put the flowerpots back after all the wind and frenzy?

Mini-World Mysteries Solutions Files

SOLUTION FILES

#1 Table Talk Mystery Solution

45 SOLUTION

Where was each person seated? *[Review all clues]*

 BILLY  OLIVIA   KELLIE

 MISSY   ZOE

 ILISH   JOSH TARA

 ALEX

46 SOLUTION

Who was involved in the mysterious bomb scare?

[JOKER – BULLY – PHOTOGRAPHER - KELLIE]

Who left the room? *[MISSY left the room]*

Who opened the window? *[ZOE opened the window]*

Who sat and laughed? *[JOSH – THE JOKER]*

47 SOLUTION

What actually was the mysterious bomb scare?
[JOKE + SILENCE + PARTY POPPER + FLASH + FART]

SOLUTION FILES

MINI WORLD MYSTERIES

#2 Scarecrow in the Vegie Patch Mystery Solution

NOTE: THIS SOLUTION CAN ALSO BE REVERSED AS IN A MIRROR IMAGE

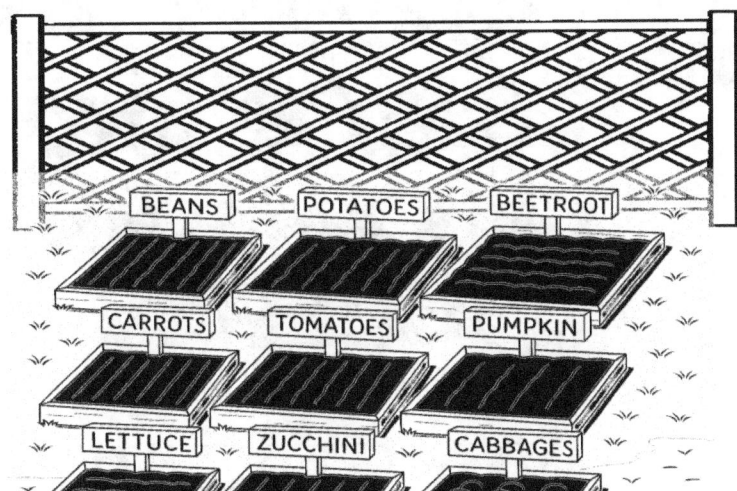

The **VEGIE PLOT** layout & positioning of **FENCE**

SOLUTION

SOLUTION FILES

Positioning of **SPRINKLER** & **COMPOST**

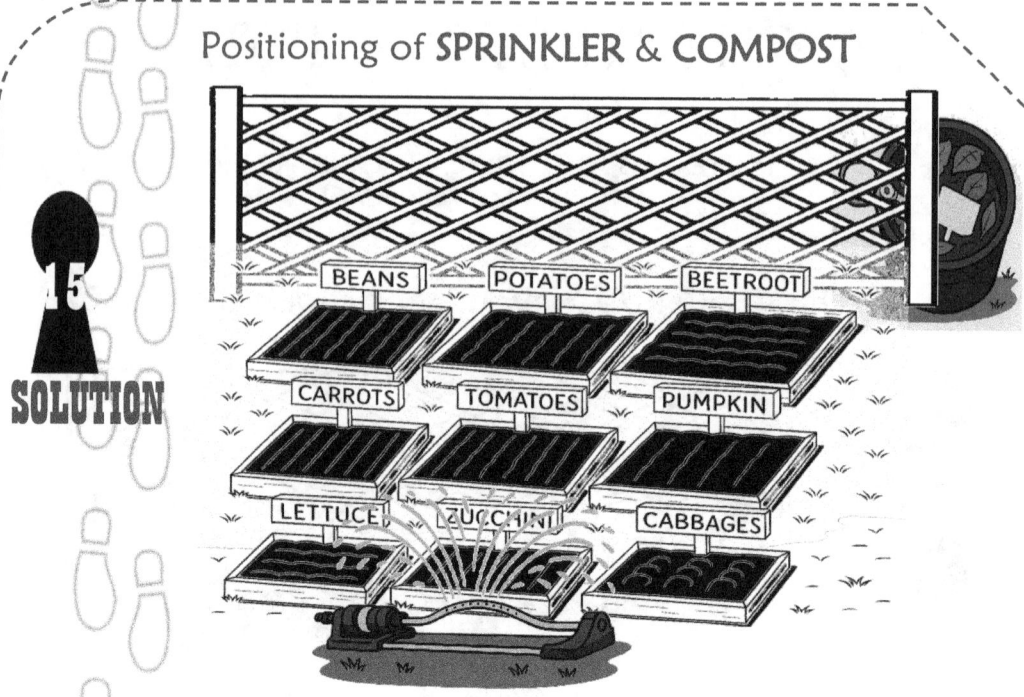

15 SOLUTION

Positioning of **SCARECROW** & **RAKE**

16 SOLUTION

MINI WORLD MYSTERIES

#3 A Walk in the Park Mystery Solution

- Recheck all your **CLUES** to verify you have all elements in their correct positions.
- Your answers should be fairly self-explanatory.

- The duck flew onto the pond and did a duck-dive.
- The ball bounced off into the grass and became lodged between a rock and the fence near the west end of the park.
- The dog & owner were walking in an easterly direction.
- The bone was not found in this scenario, as it was left at home!
- SHERLAC is an anagram of

Use a mirror

PICTORIAL SOLUTION

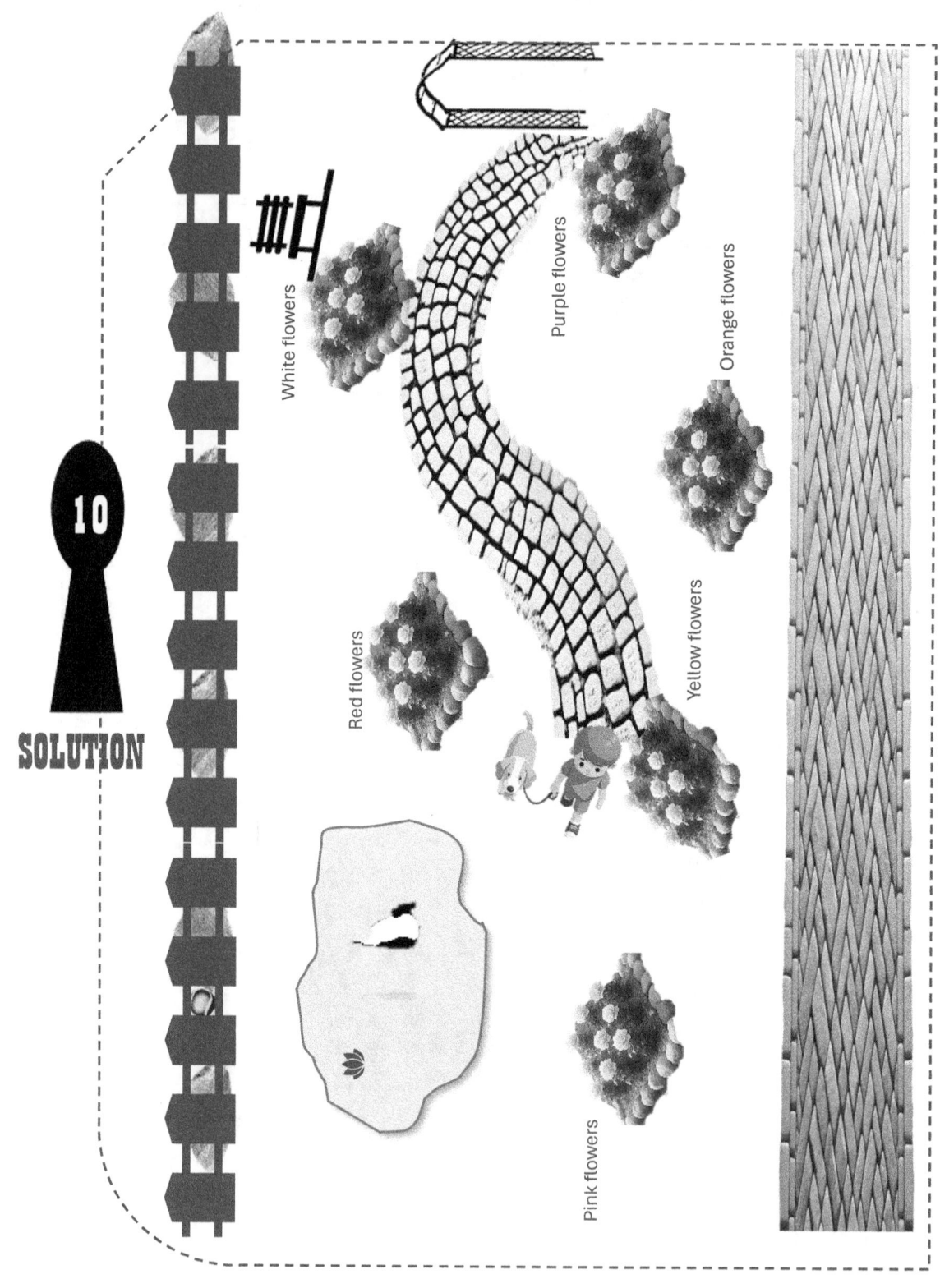

#4 K-9 Capers Mystery Solution

DOG NAMES

* BOXER: BOUNCE
* GREAT DANE: PEE WEE
* SHI TZU: MUFFIN
* PUG: SNORTY
* CHIHUAHUA: RAMBO
* ROXIE: BULL TERRIER
* TOY POODLE: MARSHMALLOW
* KING CHARLES CAVILIER: CASEY
* SCOTTISH TERRIER: SHADOW

Use a mirror to see your answers

SOLUTION FILES

PEOPLE NAMES

* TATTOOED MAN: DIESEL
* DARK SKINNED BOY: JABARI
* FLAMBOYANT WOMAN: ISADORA
* YOUNGER GIRL: BONNIE
* ASIAN LOOKING WOMAN WITH SUNNIES: JISOO
* YOUNG WOMAN ON MOBILE: AMBER
* WOMAN WEARING SHORTS AND SUNNIES: ZARA
* MAN WITH BACK PACK & MOUSTACHE: VINNIE
* OLDER WOMAN WEARING SUN-HAT: HELENA

Use a mirror to see your answers

MINI WORLD MYSTERIES

DOGS & OWNERS

* VINIE & BOUNCER
* ZARA & PEE WEE
* BONNIE & SNORTY
* ISADORA & MUFFIN
* JISOO & MARSHMALLOW
* JABARI & ROXIE
* DIESEL & SHADOW
* HELENA & CASEY
* AMBER & RAMBO

Use a mirror to see your answers

SOLUTION FILES

WHITE SIDE ANSWERS

- Every weekend VINIE & BOUNCER would go out for long hikes along the walking track.
- JISOO & MARSHMALLOW spent a lot of time at home. Marshmallow slept on the sofa next Jisoo who loved reading.
- ISADORA & MUFFIN spent all day together at the K-9 CLIPPERS. Muffin would either snooze in the corner or chew on her doggy muffin treats.

Use a mirror to see your answers

WHITE SIDE ANSWERS

- You would not expect to find Pee Wee, Casey or Marshmallow at the beach.

- Shadow was lonely and was always escaping his compound and was often seen waiting outside his owner's workplace. On more than one occasion he had been caught and taken to the Dog-Pound.

Use a mirror to see your answers

WHITE SIDE ANSWERS

- Shorty was born with a gut issue and also suffered from arthritis and so was frequently seen at the vets.
- Every Sunday morning HELEN would take CASEY to the DOG TRAINING SCHOOL.
- Rambo, Roxie, Bouncer & Pee Wee would frequently chase each other around at the park. In fact Zara and Amber had known each other from school days, and so ... the long and short of it is ... that Pee Wee and Rambo became best friends.

Use a mirror to see your answers

WHITE SIDE ANSWERS

- Zara owned a sports car. The first time she took Pee Wee for a drive — he loved it! The wind in his face and the speed. Only problem was, he was so big the police could not see Zara in the driver's seat. The police pulled them over thinking that Pee Wee was driving ... and yes they were fined because he was not wearing a seat belt!

Use a mirror to see your answers

SOLUTION FILES

MINI WORLD MYSTERIES

#5 Teddy Bears' Picnic Mishaps Mystery Solution

Blue Teddy Bear switched the ribbons, because he wanted to get back at everyone for choosing him to be 'it'.

- RED RIBBON – RED BEAR – APPLES & PEARS
- YELLOW RIBBON – YELLOW BEAR – HONEY POTS
- WHITE RIBBON – WHITE BEAR – SQUARE SANDWICHES
- MAUVE RIBBON – MAUVE BEAR – GRAPES & BANANAS
- PINK RIBBON – PINK BEAR – EASTER EGGS
- BLUE RIBBON – BLUE BEAR – CANDY & LICORICE ALLSORTS
- ORANGE RIBBON – ORANGE BEAR – TRIANGULAR SANDWICHES
- GREEN RIBBON – BROWN (GREEN BEAR) – BREAD ROLLS

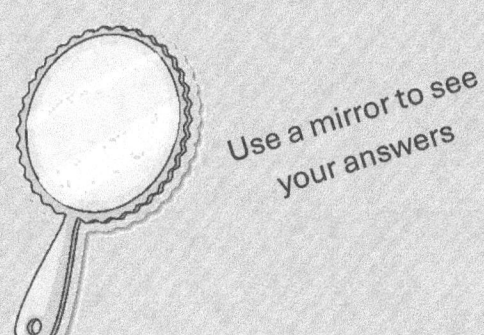

Use a mirror to see your answers

SOLUTIONS cont.

- QUEENY, was the Mauve Teddy Bear with the crown.
- The Red Teddy Bear had climbed the tree, scraped her leg/paw, and had a Band-Aid on her leg.
- The blue ribbon found on the hedge was just a decoy.
- QUEENY, was most disappointed and angry because she was a bossy perfectionist. In fact she pronounced her color mauve as 'MOVE!'.
- The Brown/Green Teddy Bear's ribbon was never switched at all, because he was Blue Teddy Bear's best buddy.
- Blue Teddy sat on the park bench.
- The Mauve Teddy Bear, the Pink Teddy Bear and the White Teddy Bear all went home without a balloon.
- Still trying to figure out who wrote the sign?! Actually ... who wrote the song?

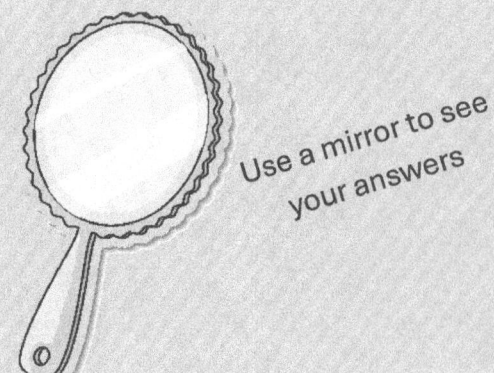

Use a mirror to see your answers

MINI WORLD MYSTERIES

The Teddy Bears' Picnic

If you go down in the woods today,
You're sure of a big surprise.
If you go down in the woods today,
You'd better go in disguise.
For every bear that ever there was
Will gather there for certain because
Today's the day the teddy bears have their picnic.

Every good little teddy bear
Is sure of a treat today.
There's lots of marvellous things to eat
And wonderful games to play.
Beneath the trees where nobody sees,
they'll hide and seek as long as they please
'Cause that's the ways the teddy bears have their picnic.

Picnic time for teddy bears.
The little teddy bears
Are having a lovely time today.
Watch them, catch them unawares
And see them picnic on their holiday.
See them gayly gad about.
They love to play and shout.
They never have any care.
At 6 o'clock, their mommies and daddies
Will take them home to bed,
Because they're tired, little teddy bears.

If you go down in the woods today,
You'd better not go alone.
It's lovely down in the woods today,
But it's safer to stay at home.
For every bear that ever there was
Will gather there for certain because
Today's the day the teddy bears have their picnic.

SOLUTIONS cont.

FINALLY ... this is for the history buffs only! Actually ... who wrote the *song*?

- In 1907, John W. Bratton, an American composer, wrote "The Teddy Bear Two-step." This version had no lyrics, but it nevertheless gained traction among the American public. In fact, one of the first recordings of the song occurred in 1907 by the Black Diamond Band.

- It took another 25 years for lyrics were added to "The Teddy Bear Two-Step." Written by Irish songwriter Jimmy Kennedy in 1932, this is the version that we know and love today.

- It was renamed "The Teddy Bears' Picnic," and it was first recorded by Henry Hall and His Orchestra, with the vocals done by Val Rosing. The song went on to be covered by several other famous singers including Bing Crosby, Rosemary Clooney, and Anne Murray.

MINI WORLD MYSTERIES

#6 The Mystery of King Azurepaw's Secret Garden Solution

- The King drank 'SHRINKING JUICE' found in his blue drinking bottle
- The two visible clues on the outside of the wall and atop the wall of his castle are weathervane & bell.
- The PASSWORD is ... 'WEATHER-BELL'.
- The King loved to sit under the shade of a large PINK tree.
- The breeze was blowing from south-to-north ... in a NORTHLY direction.
- From where the yacht is on the water, IT IS SAILING AWAY FROM THE BRIDGE

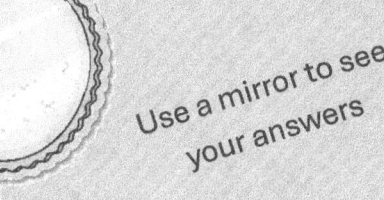

Use a mirror to see your answers

SOLUTION FILES

- The CROWN JEWEL ... was STOLEN BY THE BIRD.
- The bird dropped it into the WISHING WELL.
- The only way the King could get it back was to MAKE A WISH.
- The BIRD had landed on the MINUTE-HAND of the clock, waiting for just the right moment to swoop at the King's crown. The bird had put too much pressure on the clock hand, causing it to get stuck, although the clock mechanism was still working.
- The time that the King realised the CROWN JEWEL was missing was somewhere between 4.01 pm – 4.29 pm as he had heard 3 chimes for 3.00, one chime at 3.30 and 4 chimes for 4.00 pm
- Therefore, the Crown Jewel was stolen at 2.50 pm.

Use a mirror to see your answers

SOLUTION FILES

MINI WORLD MYSTERIES

#7 Hanging Out… On-Line Mystery Solution

HYPOTHETICAL ENDING #1

The Blame Game – Framed by Feathers

Culprits: ☐ **Penny the Purple Bird** (*Mastermind*) & ☐ **Gracie the Green Bird** (*Unwitting Accomplice*)

Twist: Penny, tired of being overlooked, secretly repositioned the vest and bloomers while no one was watching. She then dropped the rug *herself* to make it seem like Gracie's nest-stealing habits were the cause. Gracie was too focused on fluffing her feathers to notice that she was being framed.

Reveal Line: "While everyone looked at Ollie's chaos and Ruby's drama, it was *quiet Penny* who orchestrated the confusion—and left Gracie near the front row almost caught 'green-handed' holding the bloomers.

SOLUTION FILES

OPTIONAL ENDING #2

Bugged and Blown Away

Culprit: Buzz the Blowfly

Twist: It was Buzz, the black blowfly, who buzzed annoyingly too close to the birds toward the back, causing a chain reaction. It was his excitement about smelling the freshness of the washed clothing which caused havoc. His flight-path triggered the peg holding the beanie to be knocked off, causing it to fall, which in turn and startled a few birds — rousing them to shuffle around chaotically like confused dominoes. Birds flapping frantically ... clothes and pegs dropping off ... being relocated and in need of re-pegging, which in turn Miss Polly had legitimately mistaken as tampering.

Reveal Line: "Turns out the birds weren't to blame at all. It was Buzz — just doing what blowflies do. FLY ... BUZZ ... FLAP, BUMP, ANNOY and cause MAYHEM basically!"

MINI WORLD MYSTERIES

OPTIONAL ENDING #3
Teamwork with a Touch of Chaos

Culprits: ☐ Bluebell, ☐ Sunny, and ☐ Ollie

Twist: Sunny and Bluebell thought the vest looked better with their favourite colored pegs and decided to '*tidy up*'. Ollie also tried to help out but knocked the beanie off in the process. The bloomers were apparently flapping perilously in the breeze resulting in one peg falling off ... so Ollie re-pegged them randomly with the closest colors. No one actually *meant* to cause a scene — but it seems that chaos loves company.

Reveal Line: "It wasn't sabotage — it was a color-coded clean-up with clumsy consequences!"

SOLUTION FILES

FINAL THOUGHTS

- Which of these hypothetical endings were you closest to solving?
- Which of these hypotheticals offers the best solution for you?
- Maybe your team came up with different solution. If so, please write it down and share it with the PUBLISHER / AUTHOR.

By the way ... the other sock blew away with the first gust of wind and landed in Over the next door neighbour's back yard.

MINI WORLD MYSTERIES

SOLUTION as per Miss Polly's window view

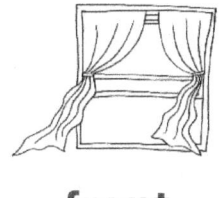

front

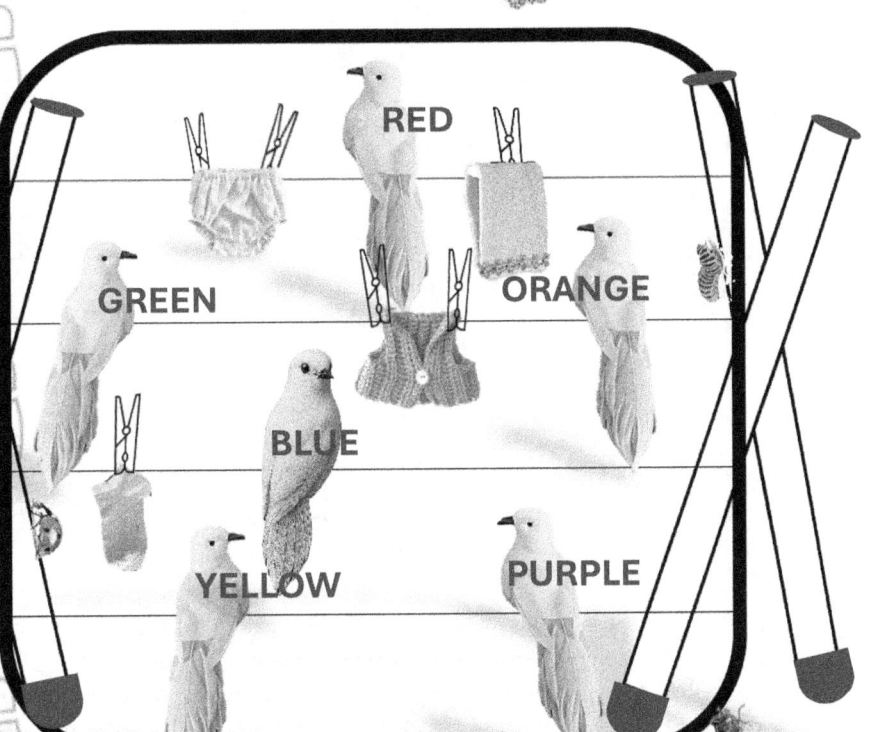

back

SOLUTION FILES

#8 Mysterious Butterfly Frenzie @ #54 Solution

SOLUTIONS

- On the outside of #54, the butterfly without the landing gear landed on the grass somewhere in between the frog and the bird.
- The gnome had dug up the carrot and the rat had tried to steal the carrot before he found the cheese.
- The bird had stolen the cheese during the gust of wind so as to lure the rat away from the carrot and set up the cat to chase after the rat.
- The frog unfortunately had gotten in the way of the gnome's shovel when the carrot was being dug up, and so consequently he positioned himself at the opposite end of the fence near the mushroom for safety.

Use a mirror to see your answers

SOLUTION FILES

SOLUTIONS cont'd.

- The cat was actually after the bird.
- If looks could be deceptive, then the bird was a real trouble maker, because she knew that the cat only had three legs, and tried to divert the cat's attention away from herself to the rat ... even though she knew he was a scavenger, and was simply trying to find food for his family.
- The fact is, that in this garden scenario everyone is innocent except for the bird and the cat.
- And the good Samaritan? Well that was ... the gnome of course. He used his trusty shovel for leverage.

Use a mirror to see your answers

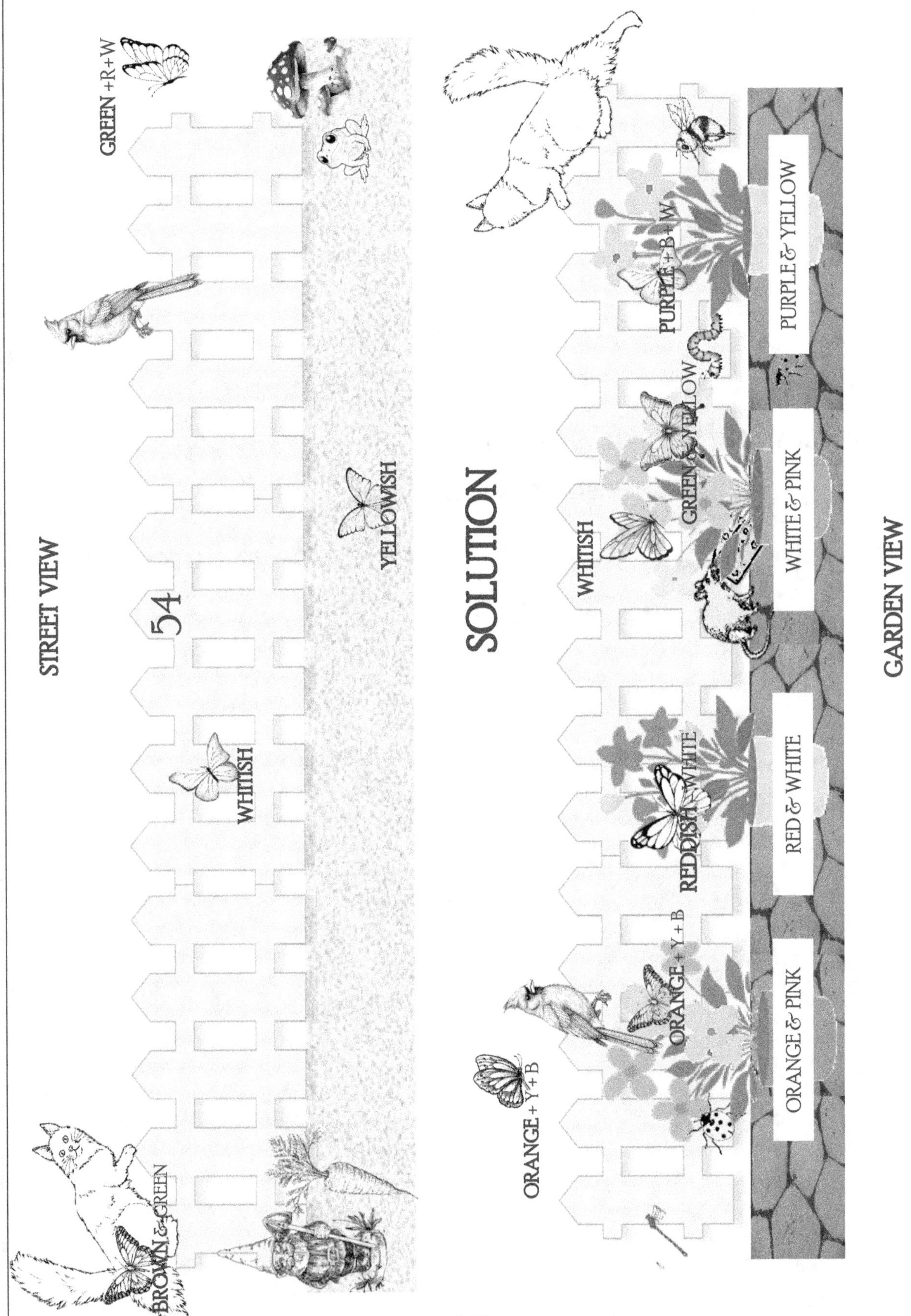

MINI WORLD MYSTERIES

STREET VIEW

GREEN +R+W

WHITISH

YELLOWISH

54

BROWN & GREEN

SOLUTION

WHITISH

PURPLE +B+W

GREEN & YELLOW

REDDISH WHITE

ORANGE + Y + B

ORANGE + Y+B

GARDEN VIEW

PURPLE & YELLOW

WHITE & PINK

RED & WHITE

ORANGE & PINK

139

BONUS OFFER

By visiting

www.gablesbooks.com

You can order a PDF document containing all the graphics for clearer printouts. This will save you time and the effort of photocopying.

This offer is only available once you have purchased your copy of the book.

www.ingramcontent.com/pod-product-compliance
Lightning Source LLC
Chambersburg PA
CBHW081400070526
44583CB00020B/2613